The Making of America

The Civil War

The Chronicle of American History from 1861 to 1865

A Bluewood Book

THE MAKING OF AMERICA:
The Civil War
by Marty Jezer

A Bluewood Book

This edition produced and published by
Bluewood Books
P.O. Box 689
San Mateo, CA 94401

ISBN 0-912517-50-6

Printed in USA

Editor: Tony Napoli
Designer: Kevin Harris
Indexer: Barbara Cross

On the cover: July 18, 1863, the 54th Massachusetts Colored Regiment charging Fort Wagner, South Carolina.

Picture Acknowledgements:
We wish to thank the following for the illustrations in this book: Bluewood Archives, Library of Congress, National Archives, National Park Service, New York Historical Society, New York Public Library, San Mateo Public Library, The White House.

Marty Jezer is a freelance writer. He has written several books, including *Opening of the Western Frontier* (1816-1860) and biographies of Rachel Carson and Abbie Hoffman. He lives in Brattleboro,Vermont and is a columnist for a local newspaper.

Also in *The Making of America Series:*
Exploration & Discovery (1492-1606)
Our Colonial Period (1607-1770)
The Revolutionary War (1770-1789)
Rise of a New Nation (1787-1815)
Opening of the Western Frontier (1816-1860)

Other titles of interest from
Bluewood Books:

100 African-Americans Who Shaped American History
100 Americans Who Shaped American History
100 Artists Who Shaped World History
100 Athletes Who Shaped Sports History
100 Authors Who Shaped World History
100 Battles That Shaped World History
100 Colonial Leaders Who Shaped North America
100 Events That Shaped World History
100 Explorers Who Shaped World History
100 Families Who Shaped World History
100 Folk Heroes Who Shaped World History
100 Great Cities of World History
100 Inventions That Shaped World History
100 Medical Milestones That Shaped World History
100 Men Who Shaped World History
100 Military Leaders Who Shaped World History
100 Natural Wonders of the World
100 Relationships That Shaped World History
100 Scientists Who Shaped World History
100 Ships and Planes That Shaped World History
100 Spiritual Leaders Who Shaped World History
100 Wars That Shaped World History
100 Women Who Shaped World History
100 World Leaders Who Shaped World History

True Stories of the Wild West
True Stories of Baseball's Hall of Famers

American Politics in the 20th Century
Media in the 20th Century
Law & Order in the 20th Century
Technology in the 20th Cenbtury

TABLE OF CONTENTS

THE SOUTH SECEDES FROM THE UNION

The 1860 election of Republican Abraham Lincoln as president catapulted the United States headlong towards a civil war. Running as an opponent of the spread of slavery into new states and territories, Lincoln won an overwhelming, though sectional, victory. Although his name was not even on the ballot in 10 Southern states, Lincoln carried 18 states, receiving 180 electoral votes and 1,866,452 popular votes.

Lincoln's Democratic opponent, Illinois Senator Stephen A. Douglas, received 1,376,957 popular votes but only the nine electoral votes of Missouri (plus three from New Jersey). Douglas campaigned on the idea of popular sovereignty, which would allow new states to choose or prohibit slavery by popular vote. Douglas's willingness to allow slavery wherever it had popular support did not satisfy the South, however. In the election of 1860, Southerners demanded the legalization of slavery in every territory and state, and nothing less.

STEPHEN DOUGLAS

The combined popular vote of the two Northern candidates, Lincoln and Douglas, exceeded the combined popular votes of the two Southern candidates, John C. Breckinridge of Kentucky and John Bell of Tennessee, by a margin of nearly two-and-a-half to one. Breckinridge, who carried the electoral votes of eleven slave states, was an ex-Democrat and James Buchanan's vice president, who insisted on the right of white people to hold slaves everywhere in the country. Bell, a former Whig who carried three border slave states, tried to avoid the slavery issue altogether, promising to uphold the law and the Constitution which, at that point, protected the rights of slaveholders everywhere in the United States.

The United States had been grappling with the issue of slavery ever since its inception. Many of the men who drafted and signed the Constitution opposed the system of slavery. They considered slavery not only to be immoral, but also so uneconomical and inefficient that it would soon die out. However, to ban slavery would have meant that the slaveholding states would have refused to ratify the Constitution. To keep the Southern states in the union, the "Three-Fifths Compromise" of the Constitution was forged.

For purposes of deciding a slave state's direct share of federal taxes as well as its representation in the House of Representatives, it was agreed that every five African–American slaves would be counted as three persons. Settlement of the troubling issue of the slave trade was postponed by a clause making it illegal for Congress to outlaw the trade before 1808.

Over time, slavery did not disappear, as some expected, for economic reasons. On the contrary, the invention of the cotton gin and the success of labor-intensive cotton and tobacco as profitable export crops led to its expansion, especially in the flat, low-land agricultural regions of the Deep South.

Opposition to slavery grew in the North, however, even as support for slavery hardened in the South. The

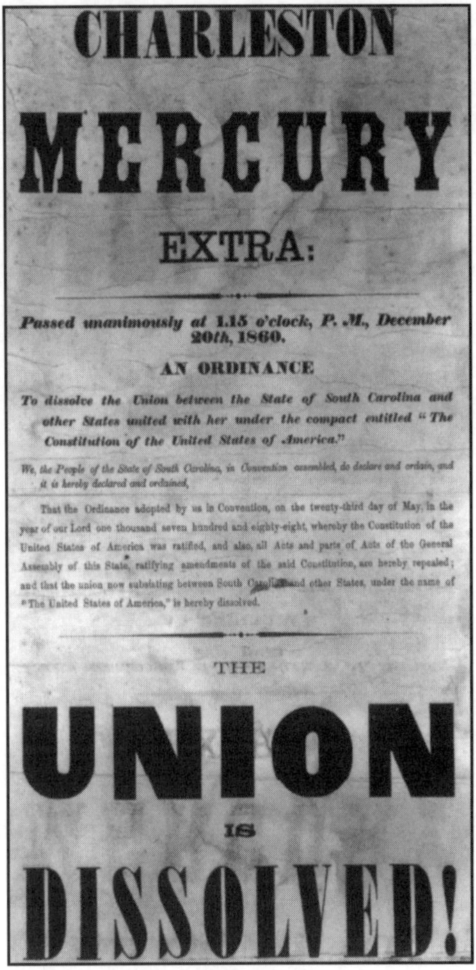

CHARLESTON

MERCURY

EXTRA:

Passed unanimously at 1.15 o'clock, P. M., December 20th, 1860.

AN ORDINANCE

To dissolve the Union between the State of South Carolina and other States united with her under the compact entitled "The Constitution of the United States of America."

We, the People of the State of South Carolina, in Convention assembled, do declare and ordain, and it is hereby declared and ordained,

That the Ordinance adopted by us in Convention, on the twenty-third day of May, in the year of our Lord one thousand seven hundred and eighty-eight, whereby the Constitution of the United States of America was ratified, and also, all Acts and parts of Acts of the General Assembly of this State, ratifying amendments of the said Constitution, are hereby repealed; and that the union now subsisting between South Carolina and other States, under the name of "The United States of America," is hereby dissolved.

THE

UNION

IS

DISSOLVED!

THE DECREE ANNOUNCING SOUTH CAROLINA'S SECESSION

Missouri Compromise of 1820 and the Kansas-Nebraska Act of 1854 were attempts to limit the expansion of slavery in the western territories while protecting its continuance where it already existed. With Lincoln's election, there could be no more give or take. He insisted that slavery was wrong, and had campaigned to stop its spread out of the slaveholding South.

Lincoln was despised by the Southern planter aristocracy that dominated Southern politics. He was viewed as course and unkempt, a symbol of Northern barbarism. A Richmond newspaper called Lincoln's election, "the greatest evil that has ever befallen this country," while in Charleston, S.C., a newspaper editorialist declared that "the tea has been thrown overboard. The Revolution of 1860 has been initiated."

Even before the election, South Carolina had threatened to secede from the Union should Lincoln win. So it was no real surprise that on December 20, 1860, the delegates to a state convention, appointed by the South Carolina legislature, voted that "the Union now subsisting between South Carolina and the other States, under the name of the 'United States of America' is hereby dissolved." Proponents of secession in the other slave states took up the cry. The secessionists believed that the South would prosper as an independent country. "Cotton, rice, tobacco, and naval stores command the world," South Carolina Senator James Hammond declared. "The North without us would be a motherless calf bleating about, and die of mange and starvation."

President James Buchanan, who remained in office until Lincoln's inauguration, March 4, 1861, lacked the political will and acumen to stem the secessionist tide. He believed that secession was unconstitutional but was reluctant to assert federal authority to stop it. In addition, as a lame duck president waiting for his term to expire, he was not in any political position to assert his control. Members of Congress also sought to find a compromise solution to defuse the crisis. However, the slave states wanted slavery to be protected everywhere, something that the Northern states opposed. No longer was there any room for compromise.

Throughout the month of January 1861, before Lincoln took office, state conventions in Georgia, Alabama, Florida, Mississippi, and Louisiana followed South Carolina's lead in voting for secession. The votes in these six states were by convention, with delegates chosen not by popular vote, but by the members of each state legislature. In these states, 854 men were delegated to decide on secession. Though only five percent of the Southern people were actual slaveholders, the majority of these delegates owned slaves. The combined vote of the six state conventions was 697 for secession, 157 against.

In all six secessionist states, the delegates justified their actions by arguing that the original 13 states had come together to create the Union; hence, individual states could vote to leave the Union. Opponents of this theory of states' rights insisted that the people as a whole had forged the Union and only the will of the people, North and South, could cause it to dissolve.

The idea of states' rights rested as much on opportunism as it did on principle. Politicians in the North and the South advocated it whenever it suited their sectional advantage. The right of states to secede from the Union was first advanced by New Englanders who wanted to negotiate a settlement with England rather than continue to fight the

War of 1812. Southerners became states' righters during the Jacksonian Era in opposition to a protective tariff, and then adapted the theory to the defense of slavery. In the period before the 1860 election, a few Northern states used the states' rights theory to uphold their refusal to enforce the Fugitive Slave Law, insisting that individual states had the right to disobey what they considered an "unjust" federal law. In this instance, Southern leaders denounced the states' rights position and insisted upon the primacy of federal law.

The secessionist movement reflected divisions between North and South that went beyond the argument over slavery. Compared to the North, the South saw itself as homogeneous in its ethnic make-up. There were few immigrants in the South, and few Catholics and Jews. By ignoring the four million African slaves, the South could believe itself to be a purely white, Anglo-Saxon Protestant country.

Southern proponents of slavery and secession argued that their system of slavery was a more civilized system of labor than the work-for-wage system of the industrial North. Indeed, the low-pay and long-hours of the Northern factory system made workers seem like "wage-slaves," as Southerners charged. However, Northern workers were free to leave their jobs and move West if that is what they desired. The men among them could also vote. African-American slaves not only could not vote, but they were considered property rather than people, to be bought and sold by their masters who had absolute legal control over every aspect of their lives.

SAM HOUSTON

Secessionist leaders in the South believed that immigrants and working people in the North would have no stake in fighting to abolish slavery or to preserve the Union. They also believed that the rural West would side with the agrarian South against the industrial North. Some secessionists even thought that the North would be glad to rid itself of the slaveholding South and not put up a fight against the secessionist movement.

Not all slaveholders were enthusiastic about secession. Many had financial and social ties to the North and, at the beginning at least, a realistic sense of the North's overwhelming economic advantage. Jefferson Davis of Mississippi and Alexander H. Stephens of Georgia, who would soon become president and vice president of the Confederate States of America, initially pleaded for caution. They wanted to wait for Lincoln to show his hand and actually move against slavery before breaking with the Union.

In Texas, Governor Sam Houston, a hero of Texas independence, warned the secessionist forces that "You may, after the sacrifice of countless millions of treasure and hundreds of thousands of lives, as a bare possibility, win South independence. . . .But I doubt it." The North, he said, "is determined to preserve this Union...." and will move to do so "with the steady momentum and perseverance of an avalanche." Houston's views proved to be unpopular and he was deposed as governor. On February 1, Texas became the seventh state to vote for secession. Ultimately, secession was a popular movement. The people "are wild with passion and frenzy, doing what they know not what," bemoaned Alexander Stephens.

Jefferson Davis

On February 8, 1861 a convention of the seven seceded states met in Montgomery, Alabama and declared themselves the Confederate States of America (CSA) with Davis and Stephens appointed provisional president and vice-president pending formal elections. Davis saw the conflict with the North as something more than a war to preserve slavery and uphold secession. Opposition to slavery, Davis believed, was "an engine of Northern aggrandizement," a means "to promote the industry of the United States at the expense of the people of the South."

Planter, soldier, congressman, senator and an effective secretary of war during the administration of Franklin Pierce, Jefferson Davis was a man of experience and accomplishment. However, he was also stiff, formal, and always certain of his own opinions. Sam Houston, for example, described him as "cold as a lizard," while Davis's wife acknowledged that "he did not know the arts of a politician and would not practice them if understood." Though comfortable in the circles of the Southern planter aristocracy, Davis lacked the leadership qualities that appealed to the common man.

The Confederate Constitution, drafted in Montgomery, not only upheld the right of slavery, but it made that right permanent. The document prohibited Confederate legislators from having a change-of-heart and voting it out, or in any other way interfering with "the right of property in Negro slaves."

The Confederate Constitution also called for a six year term for president and, nodding towards the parliamentary system of England, gave each cabinet member a seat in Congress. It also forbade a protective tariff, as well as "internal improvements," those national canal and road building projects that in earlier days Southern leaders such as John C. Calhoun had been eager to support.

At his inauguration, on February 18, 1861, in the chosen Confederate capital, Montgomery, Alabama, Davis described the new country as "sanctified by its justice." Vice President Alexander H. Stephens was more blunt. The Confederate States of America, "is founded on the opposite idea of the quality of the races," he said. "Its cornerstone rests upon the great truth that the Negro is not equal to the white man."

PRESIDENT LINCOLN

Unlike Davis, President-elect Abraham Lincoln had no record of accomplishment and a public image of being awkward and homely. He also had a modesty that contrasted with Davis' self-confident and aristocratic bearing. "Ladies and gentlemen, I am glad to see you," Lincoln would often begin his speeches. "I suppose you are to see me, but I certainly think I have the best of the bargain." However, Lincoln also had a reputation for being firm and honest. He had vowed to stop the spread of slavery and saw that conflict with the South over this issue was inevitable. "Hold firm, as with a chain of steel," he said during the election campaign. "The tug has to come, and better now than any time hereafter."

Unable to act between his election and his inauguration, Lincoln spoke in general terms about preserving the Union, but did not interfere in the way that outgoing President Buchanan dealt with the crisis. Lincoln believed that only the slaveholders supported secession, and that if he remained firm in favor of the Union and did not threaten Southern institutions, the secessionist tide would run its course and the South would recommit itself to the Union.

In February, Davis sent Stephens and two other commissioners to Washington to attempt to negotiate a peaceful resolution. Stephens and Lincoln had been friends when they were both in Congress, but now Lincoln refused to meet with the Confederate delegates so as not to legitimize the legality of their position.

Washington D.C. bordered on Virginia and Maryland, two states with many Confederate sympathizers. When Lincoln left Illinois to travel to Washington for his inauguration, he had to be spirited secretly through Baltimore because of rumors of an assassination plot against him. In his inaugural address, Lincoln took a firm stand against secession. "In your hands, my dissatisfied fellow countrymen, and not in mine, is the momentous issue of civil war. The government will not assail you. You can have no conflict without being yourself the aggressors. You have no oath registered in heaven to destroy the government, while I shall have the most solemn one to 'preserve, protect and defend' it."

MAJOR ROBERT ANDERSON

Lincoln also tried to reach out to those Southerners torn or ambivalent about the secessionist course. "We are not enemies," Lincoln said, "but friends. We must not be enemies. Though passion may have strained, it must not break our bonds of affection."

However, already events were spiraling towards armed confrontation. During January and February, federal army and navy installations in the South were quietly turned over to secessionist forces without any protest from President Buchanan. An exception was South Carolina's Fort Sumter, guarding the entrance to Charleston's harbor. Because that state was the leader of the secessionist movement, the fort had a symbolic value that exceeded its military importance. In response to South Carolina's secession, Major Robert Anderson, the Union commander of Fort Moultrie, another federal installation in Charleston harbor, relocated the 68 men under his command to nearby Fort Sumter to better protect them from a Southern provocation. Anderson, a Kentuckian who had once held slaves, remained loyal to the Union.

When Lincoln took office, the fort was low on supplies, so something had to be done. Most of his cabinet advised the president to avoid confrontation and turn the fort over to South Carolina. General Winfield Scott, a hero of the Mexican War and the highest ranking general in the U.S. Army, advised Lincoln that it would take a major military effort—a large naval fleet and 25,000 troops—to resupply the outpost.

Lincoln tried to find a middle ground. He advised Confederate authorities that he intended to send a ship to resupply the fort, but that the ship would not carry either arms or reinforcements. The Confederate cabinet was split in terms of how to react. Secretary of State Robert Toombs advised Davis against military action. Firing at Fort Sumter "is suicide, murder, and will lose us every friend in the North. It will also stir the people of the North to take up arms. It is unnecessary; it puts us in the wrong; it is fatal," he said. However, other secessionists believed that a confrontation would rally the South and lead Virginia and the border states to quit the Union and join the Confederacy.

At midnight on April 12, four representatives of the Confederacy rowed out to Fort Sumter and told Major Anderson that he had until 4 a.m. to surrender. Anderson refused, and later that day, the South Carolina militia opened fire. The honor of firing the first canon was given to a Virginia Congressman, Roger Pryor, who had boldly advocated the attack. However, Pryor couldn't bring himself to "fire the first shot of the war," so the privilege went to Edmund Ruffin, a colleague of John C. Calhoun who had been advocating secession for 20 years. The Confederate artillery was commanded by General P.G.T. Beauregard, who had learned artillery from Major Anderson when Anderson was an instructor at West Point. Except for a horse, there were no casualties in either the Confederate bombardment or the Union response; after 34 hours, with ammunition running low, Anderson surrendered the fort.

On April 14, a Confederate flag flew high above Fort Sumter. The South had won the first battle of the Civil War.

THE CONFEDERATE FLAG FLIES ABOVE FORT SUMTER, APRIL 14,1861

FROM FORT SUMTER TO BULL RUN

The firing on Fort Sumter inspired an outpouring of patriotic sentiment in both the North and the South. The tension of drift and indecision was over. There was relief on both sides that the conflict was now out in the open. That the firing on Fort Sumter had cost no lives—except in the aftermath, when during the ceremony of surrender a powder charge accidentally exploded, killing two Union soldiers—added to the feeling of nationalistic celebration. War would finally settle the issue, though few foresaw how bloody and costly it would be.

The United States in 1861 did not have a large standing army. Before secession, it consisted of fewer than 17,000 professional soldiers, most of them stationed in the West. Each state had its own militia, but they were ill-equipped and poorly trained. With the firing on Fort Sumter, the South was now in armed rebellion. Lincoln would have to build an army fast. Two days after the surrender of Fort Sumter, Lincoln called on the states to send him 75,000 militia men for three months service. He and his advisors still believed that a quick show of force would put an end to the Confederate uprising.

The response to Lincoln's call was overwhelming. New York State alone voted to supply 30,000 men for three years duty. The governor of Iowa telegraphed Lincoln, "For God's sake send us arms. We have the men." Many states had to be discouraged from immediately sending militia to Washington, which was unprepared to house and feed them. Whatever Northerners thought about slavery, they were outraged at the Confederate attack

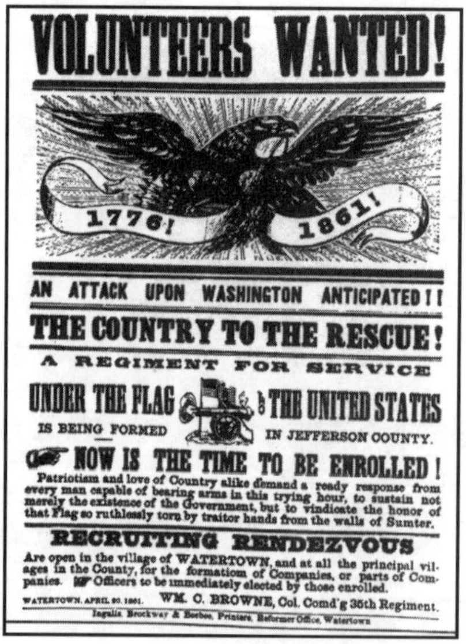

A CALL FOR VOLUNTEERS TO SERVE IN THE UNION ARMY

and rallied to Lincoln's call to save the Union.

The South also reacted quickly. On April 17, a convention of delegates voted to secede and join the Confederacy, subject to a vote by the people in an election in May. To encourage secession, Confederate leaders named Richmond as their new capital. Two days later, Lincoln declared a blockade of all Southern ports. The next day, before the blockade could be imposed, a small unit of Virginian troops moved against the federal naval base in Norfolk, Virginia and captured it without a fight. Lincoln had refrained from reinforcing the base in the hope of keeping Virginia in the Union. Now Virginia was lost, along with weapons, munitions, and a number of ships.

The Confederate capitol in Richmond, Virginia

The Union navy was very small, but the seafaring New England states had the shipbuilding infrastructure to speed construction of a new navy. By the summer, Union naval squadrons were patrolling offshore of all the Southern shipping ports. Some 50,000 Confederate soldiers had to be stationed in Southern ports to prevent Union landings. In the first year of the blockade, sailings to and from the Confederate ports dropped from 6,000 before the war to about 800.

The Confederates passed a law mandating that all foreign ships that entered Southern ports had to include armaments in its cargo. The Confederate army was clothed, for the most part, in garments imported from England. To pay for this, the South had to get its exports of cotton, rice, tobacco, and forest products through the blockade. As the war continued, the Union navy effectively curtailed trade in and out of Southern ports. The Confederates bought a fleet of small, speedy blockade-runners from England, but by 1864 an estimated one out of three was getting caught.

Lincoln's first choice to command the Union army was a Virginian, Robert E. Lee. Lee had served in the Mexican War, and from 1852 to 1855 was superintendent of the U.S. Military Academy at West Point. Lee had long believed that slavery was an evil. He had freed his own slaves and believed that the South would do better economically if

GENERAL ROBERT E. LEE

slave labor was prohibited. He also opposed Virginia's vote for secession. However, he felt loyal to his friends, his family, and his state. "I can contemplate no greater calamity for the country than a dissolution of the Union. . . . Still, a Union that can only be maintained by swords and bayonets, and in which strife and civil war are to take the place of brotherly love and kindness has no charm for me," he wrote his son. On April 23, Lee accepted the command of the Confederate army in Virginia. "I cannot raise my hand against my birthplace, my home, my children," he wrote to a Northern friend.

In early May, Arkansas followed Virginia in joining the Confederacy. Tennessee and North Carolina followed thereafter, although the people and members of Congress from the mountainous regions of eastern Tennessee remained loyal to the federal government.

The Border States—Maryland, Missouri, and Kentucky—were in a unique situation. All three allowed slavery, and all three had both Southern and Northern sympathizers. Lincoln's emphasis on holding the Union together, as opposed to rallying citizens in a crusade against slavery, kept the border states aligned with the federal government. However, the president was also not above using force if necessary to ensure the loyalty of these crucial states. In Maryland, for example, the federal government imprisoned the pro-Confederate leadership and thus held the state for the Union. Missouri's governor, Claiborne F. Jackson, supported the South, while the legislature supported the Union. Only after the intervention by Union forces, and battles at Wilson's Creek in August 1861 and Pea Ridge in March 1862, was Missouri secured for the Union. Kentucky first declared its neutrality, though the legislature ultimately pledged support for the Union.

The South itself had its share of Northern sympathizers. In the hill country of eastern Tennessee, Northern

Alabama, and in the mountains of northwestern Virginia, where the rugged terrain prevented the plantation system from taking root, small farmers had no use for slavery or for the aristocratic slaveholders who dominated state government. When Virginia seceded from the Union, its northwestern counties refused to go along. In 1863, these 50 counties were admitted into the Union as the state of West Virginia.

The Civil War brought strife to families as well. Three of Mrs. Lincoln's brothers died fighting for the Confederacy, while relatives of Mrs. Jefferson Davis fought for the North. Robert E. Lee's cousin, Samuel P. Lee, fought against him as commander of the Union naval forces operating on the James River. Major General T.L. Crittenden of the Union army was the brother of Major General G.B. Crittenden of the Confederate army.

Samuel P. Lee

In terms of manpower, the North had an overwhelming advantage. The South had a population of under 6 million (plus about 4 million slaves) against the North's more than 19 million. Historians disagree about the number of enlistments in each of the two armies, but the figures are approximately 1.5 million for the North and about 800,000 for the South. The North had an overwhelming economic advantage as well, with more than 100,000 factories to the South's 20,600; 1,100,000 industrial workers to the South's 111,000; and 20,000 miles of railroad track to the South's 9,000. With the exception of exports crops such as cotton, rice and tobacco, all of which were based on the plantation system's exploitation of slave labor, the South could not compete with Northern and midwestern agriculture. In the production of grains, vegetables, livestock, dairy products, cattle fodder and feed, the Union had a tremendous advantage.

The South made up for its lack of men and resources with a strategic advantage. The North had to decisively defeat the South in order to bring it back into the Union and, at the same time, resolve the slavery issue to its satisfaction. All the South had to do was to continue fighting and prolong the war. The Confederacy's leaders felt they did not have to defeat the North in many battles; they only had to make Northerners tire of the war so that they would want to negotiate a settlement. Simply by having an army on the battlefield, the Confederates forced the Northerners into attacking them. The

THE UNION ARMY'S DEFENSES LINE THE POTOMAC RIVER

Union forces had to go on the offensive; Confederate troops could stay in the South, near their resources, and force the Northern armies to come after them. This meant the North had to transport supplies and troops into the South and these supply lines were vulnerable to attack.

The Confederacy could fight a defensive war. Its target, in a sense, was Northern public opinion. The South hoped that Union casualties would make the war politically unpopular and force Lincoln to sue for peace on terms that the South deemed acceptable. Because the North had to attack the South, the South was also able to perceive itself as defending its own territory. The North, in this sense, was the aggressor, invading Southern territory. This fact was important in rallying the people of the South. To the majority of Southerners who owned no slaves, the war became a campaign to protect their land and heritage against an invading army.

The South also had a geographic advantage. Washington, D.C. was across the Potomac River from Virginia, while Maryland bordered the capital on its other three sides. In Maryland, Confederate sympathizers blew up railroads and telegraph lines in order to cut Washington off from the rest of the North. The capital had few troops to protect it. Massachusetts militia men had to battle Confederate sympathizers as they passed through Baltimore on their way to Washington. So strong was Southern sentiment in the areas around Washington, that Lincoln suspended the right of habeas corpus in Maryland, sent federal troops to occupy Baltimore, and imprisoned secessionist members of the state legislature, as well as various Baltimore city officials; they were kept in jail until the Unionists got things under control. On April 25, Northern troops began to arrive to defend the capital city.

Lincoln was very concerned about protecting Washington from a Virginian army. On May 23, after Virginia had voted for secession by a margin of three to one, Union troops crossed the Potomac and established fortifications in Arlington and Alexandria in order to protect the capital. Lincoln also sent

Major General George McClellan with 20,000 Ohio volunteers to support Union sympathizers in the northwestern counties. In the town of Philippi, in present-day West Virginia, McClellan found a small Confederate force asleep and forced them to flee into the night, with only one casualty of his own. He then defeated a small Confederate army of 4,500 men at the mountain pass between Rich and Laurel Mountains near Beverly, pushing them back into the Shenandoah Valley. A cautious general, McClellan allowed the Confederates to get away and regroup. However, in his dispatches to Washington, McClellan boasted of how he and his men had "annihilated two armies. . . entrenched in mountain fastness." The presence of troops to defend Washington and McClellan's inflated reports from western Virginia bolstered Union confidence that victory would be theirs, quick and easy.

General Winfield Scott told Lincoln that it would take an army of 300,000 men two or three years to capture the Confederate capital of Richmond and subdue the upper South. Scott expected to utilize the first year training and supplying a professional army. However, events created their own momentum and schedule.

The volunteers who answered Lincoln's initial call for troops were committed to serve for three months. Their enlistment period was running down. The Northern press, meanwhile, clamored for action and victory. Horace Greeley, the influential editor of the *New York Tribune*, led the cry for battle. "Forward to Richmond," his newspaper demanded.

Against the advice of his generals, who knew that the volunteers were unprepared for actual battle, Lincoln gave into popular pressure and ordered Brigadier General Irvin McDowell, the commander of the troops protecting Washington, to move against the Confederate army, some 20,000 troops under the command of Brigadier General P.G.T. Beauregard. These forces were dug in behind Bull Run, a little creek running through Manassas Junction, a railroad intersection 25 miles from Washington along the route to Richmond. The Union army was "green" Lincoln acknowledged, but so were the

UNION TROOPS OCCUPY GENERAL LEE'S HOME IN ARLINGTON, VIRGINIA

GENERAL P.G.T. BEAUREGARD

Confederates. "You are all green alike," Lincoln told McDowell.

On July 16, 1861 McDowell began to move his army of 35,000 men across the Potomac into Virginia. Many of the men were in the last days of their three-month enlistments and anxious to get home. Except for a few old veterans of the Mexican War, none had ever been in battle. Discipline was lax. Movement was slow. In addition, behind the army came several hundred civilians, carrying blankets and picnic baskets, anxious to witness the one battle that, they believed, would end the Confederate rebellion.

The Confederate troops were as inexperienced as those of the Union army but, knowing that the Union forces were coming, they were able to secure themselves a strong defensive position. Another Confederate army of 9,000 men commanded by General Joseph E. Johnston was situated at Harper's Ferry, just across the river from Maryland. Johnston's army was held in check by 16,000 troops led by Major General Robert Patterson. He had orders to put pressure on Johnston to prevent him from moving South and reinforcing Beauregard at Manassas Junction. However, Johnston faked an attack of his own and Patterson set up a defensive position. As Patterson was shoring up his defense, Johnston slipped

THE FIRST BATTLE OF BULL RUN

away from Harper's Ferry and headed for Manassas Junction.

The first Battle of Bull Run took place on July 21. Beauregard's inexperienced forces failed to accomplish a flanking maneuver, while McDowell succeeded in getting a portion of his troops across Bull Run and in position to attack the left flank of Beauregard's army. However, the Confederates held long enough for Johnston's troops to arrive from Harper's Ferry. At a point when the Confederate defense seemed as if it was breaking, Brigadier General Barnard Bee rallied his troops by pointing to a brigade of reinforcements, led by Brigadier General Thomas J. Jackson, who were pouring fire into the Union attackers. "There is Jackson, standing like a stone wall," Bee supposedly shouted, as he urged his men to gather behind him. Jackson's troops stopped the Union attack and turned the tide of battle. Jackson thereafter became known as Stonewall Jackson.

Major General George B. McClellan

The Union offensive disintegrated and McDowell ordered a withdrawal. The Union forces began an orderly retreat, until they ran into the civilian picnickers. That's when the Union army ceased to exist as a fighting force. Civilians and soldiers fled towards Washington; soon, there was chaos and confusion, as disorganized troops and panicked civilians clogged the highway. Mounted men tried to ride around them, and wheeled vehicles became tangled in the mess. Had the Confederates been able to maintain their attack, they might have destroyed McDowell's army and even captured Washington. However, the Confederate units were nearly as confused and disorganized in victory as the Union forces were in defeat. The Confederates remained in camp, sending out cavalry to pick up a large quantity of weapons left on the battlefield.

The first Battle of Bull Run put an end to the Union's confidence in a quick, bloodless victory. The number of dead, wounded, and missing was 2,896 for the Union, 1,982 for the Confederates. Lincoln, who was in despair, nevertheless moved fast to rally the country. Maintain the blockade of Southern ports, he ordered, and transform the volunteer army into a disciplined well-trained force with long-term enlistees. To do this he fired McDowell and replaced him with General McClellan, the hero of western Virginia.

During the summer, men and supplies poured into Washington. By September, the Union Army of the Potomac had 168,000 men, all encamped and in training around Washington.

VICTORY IN THE WEST, DEFEAT IN THE EAST

Bull Run forced President Lincoln to realize that the war would be long and hard, and that the Union could not depend on untrained volunteer troops. The three-month militia-men were sent home, and a new army was recruited on the basis of three-year terms. All through the winter, uniforms, weapons, and ammunition poured into the capital city as Northern industry retooled for war. However, Lincoln still had to rely on the individual states for recruiting the soldiers. The governor of each state was given titular command of his state's army. The regiments were commanded by state leaders, many of

GENERAL WINFIELD SCOTT WITH HIS STAFF

whom were political appointees with no military experience. Only when the state units were at full strength did the soldiers become part of the Union army. Still, the inexperience and, in some cases, incompetence of the politically appointed officers consistently undermined the Union's military effort.

McClellan proved to be an excellent organizer and popular with the soldiers training in Washington. A veteran of the Mexican War who had returned to the army after spending time as a railroad executive, McClellan was also vain, ambitious, and arrogant. He disdained Lincoln and was ambitious to replace him as the nation's leader. Still, Lincoln was impressed by McClellan's training efforts. So when it became apparent that Winfield Scott was too old to lead the Union military effort, in November 1861, Lincoln elevated McClellan to commander-in-chief, while keeping him as the ranking field general of the Washington-based Army of the Potomac.

Though pressure again built to put the army into action, McClellan refused to go on the offensive, believing that the Confederates in Virginia were stronger than they actually were. McClellan's intelligence service estimated that the Confederates had 150,000 men defending Richmond when, in reality, they numbered only 50,000, and their arms were inadequate. McClellan's caution seemed justified, however, when a unit of Union troops, ordered to reconnoiter Confederate encampments on the Virginia side of the Potomac, blundered into well-led rebel forces and were quickly routed with heavy casualties. The Battle of Balls Bluff, though an isolated skirmish, seemed like Bull Run all over again with the Confederates triumphant.

Thaddeus Stevens

As a result, impatient members of Congress, led by radical Republicans, set up a Joint Committee on the Conduct of the War to monitor the conduct of Union generals and the war policies of the Lincoln administration. The leaders of the radicals were Representative Thaddeus Stevens of Pennsylvania and Senator Benjamin F. Wade of Ohio. They wanted to free the slaves and were anxious to carry the war into the Southern heartland. Their abolitionism, however, was a minority position, in the country as well as in the Congress.

Confederate forces in Virginia and the Washington area seemed stronger than

QUAKER GUN

but only from a distance. The South had withheld cotton exports from the European market in the hope of creating a shortage and getting higher prices for their most important export commodity. However, Europe had a surplus of cotton—and was even selling some of it to the North—so the South was unable to purchase the weapons it needed. Over time, the South, like the North, would create its own weapon industry and build a well-armed national army; but at the start of the war, Confederate soldiers were often armed with the hunting rifles they brought with them from home. These rifles were neither powerful nor accurate, and they were awkward to reload after each shot was fired.

they actually were. After Bull Run, General Joseph Johnston strengthened his defensive line around Manassas in order to stop another Union move against Richmond. Short of weapons, he built wooden guns—called "Quaker guns"— that looked like the real thing,

As the war continued, soldiers in both armies were issued Springfield rifles. These, too, were muzzle-loaded but also powerful. They could kill at a distance of one mile, although they were accurate at a range of 200 to 250 yards. A trained soldier could get two shots off in a minute, which was enough to give the defense an advantage in any frontal battle.

TROOPS IN BOTH ARMIES USED SPRINGFIELD RIFLES

General Ulysses S. Grant

Troops charging in an open field —which was the most common infantry tactic at the time—had no chance against a well dug-in opposition. Though the attacking troops were armed with bayonets, in Civil War battles the attacking army rarely had the opportunity to use them. Artillery, which fired a deadly spray of 200–300 lead slugs, made frontal assaults unfeasible, something Civil War generals didn't understand until late in the war, after thousands of troops had been slaughtered in attacks against artillery barrages. The way for attacking armies to avoid this carnage was to attempt flanking assaults against the far ends of the defending armies. This was a difficult maneuver for untrained armies; woodland, swamps, and rough terrain made it even harder.

While Washington was focused on the armies encamped around the capital and Richmond, real fighting broke out in the West, as both sides fought to gain control of the border states and to keep the Mississippi River open.

Ulysses S. Grant had been an officer in the Mexican War, but his life had then gone downhill. Forced to resign his commission because of drunkenness, he took up, without success, farming, real estate, and clerking. After Fort Sumter he enlisted as a colonel of an Illinois regiment. Because the army was short of officers with actual combat experience, Grant was quickly promoted to Brigadier General and sent to Cairo, Illinois to serve under Major General Henry W. Halleck, a good administrator with no aptitude for leading men in battle.

In the summer of 1861, the Confederates began to build earthen forts along the Mississippi River and its tributaries in order to prevent Union armies in the Midwest from invading the South through the Mississippi Valley. Two of the most important forts were Fort Henry and Fort Donelson, protect-

The Battle of Fort Donelson

ing access to the Cumberland and Tennessee rivers. Grant saw that if he could capture these forts, he would gain control of central Tennessee and gain access to Northern Alabama and Mississippi. With Halleck's reluctant approval, Grant planned his campaign. On February 7, 1862, a flotilla of gunboats commanded by James B. Eads captured Fort Henry. Grant then moved on Fort Donelson and, correctly judging that the Confederates were low on supplies, withstood bitter fighting in order to keep them hemmed in. Within three days, the Confederates surrendered.

Major General Henry Halleck

After what had happened the previous year at Bull Run, these victories were great morale boosters for the North. Grant wanted to pursue the retreating Confederates, but Halleck split his force, sending one unit, commanded by Major General John General Pope, to capture Island Number 10 on the Mississippi River, south of where the Ohio River enters. At the same time Halleck sent Grant to clear Tennessee of the Confederates. On April 6, Grant and his troops were encamped in an unfortified position at Pittsburg Landing on the Tennessee River near what is now Shiloh, Tennessee. They were attacked by the combined forces of Generals Beauregard, Leonidas Polk and Albert Sidney Johnston and almost overrun in 12 hours of fierce fighting in which Johnston was killed. The next day, with the Confederates holding the key position at Shiloh Church, Grant rallied his troops and, with reinforcements that had just arrived from Ohio, drove the Confederates back to Corinth, Mississippi.

The battle of Shiloh was fought in the driving rain, and Grant's army was, for the moment, too exhausted to pursue. The casualties were horrendous. Out of a force of 63,000 Union soldiers, 13,000 were killed or wounded. The South lost 11,000 of its 40,000 man army. Shiloh was the bloodiest battle fought on American soil up until that time. Because of the Union losses on the first day of battle, Grant was severely criticized by the Northern press as an incompetent, even as a drunk. Halleck removed him from command and, instead of pushing the attack as Grant would have done, let the Confederate army retreat into Mississippi. Lincoln, however, took note of Grant's determination. "I can't spare this man," he told Halleck. "He fights."

Admiral David G. Farragut

The removal of Confederate forces from their river fortresses allowed Union gunboats to proceed down the Mississippi from Cairo to Memphis. The American naval blockade, meanwhile, had successfully stopped Confederate shipping in and out of New Orleans. At the end of April, a Union fleet of 8 steam-driven sloops-of-war and 15 small gunboats, commanded by Rear Admiral David G. Farragut, daringly ran the gauntlet of Confederate forts below New Orleans and captured the city. His armada then sailed north, capturing other Southern fortresses along the Mississippi. Only one Confederate fortress, Vicksburg, Mississippi, held out. Otherwise the Mississippi River and all its tributaries from the Gulf of Mexico north to the Ohio River were in Union hands.

Meanwhile in the East, McClellan began to plan a new offensive. His plan was to move his army from the vicinity of the capital, outflank Confederate General Joseph E. Johnston, whose army was camped in Manassas, and proceed up the peninsula to get at Richmond. However, when Johnston abandoned Manassas and moved his army to

Fredericksburg to block him, McClellan refrained from engagement and diverted part of his army to Manassas and then back to Washington; in the end, McClellan's forces fought no battles and took no territory, except for Manassas, which Johnston had abandoned.

Impatient with McClellan's reluctance to do battle and under pressure from the radical Republicans to take the offensive, Lincoln stripped him of his supreme command and ordered him to lead the Army of the Potomac against Richmond. Until July, when Lincoln appointed Henry Halleck commander-in-chief of the Union army, Lincoln and his new War Secretary, Edwin Stanton, ran the war. Lincoln gave McClellan two options: a frontal assault, as was tried in the Battle of Bull Run, or a flanking attack from the east up the peninsula between the York and James River.

McClellan chose the peninsular route and on March 17, 1862, he began moving his troops out of the Union base in Alexandria, Virginia, across the Potomac from Washington. In so doing, McClellan ignored Lincoln's orders to keep a part of his army in Washington to stop a Confederate attack. McClellan did not believe such an attack would be forthcoming, and was more concerned with his overall troop strength. However, Lincoln was concerned with protecting Washington, and understood that a successful Confederate raid in or around the capital would demoralize the North and be a political disaster.

THE* MONITOR *FOUGHT THE* MERRIMACK/VIRGINIA *IN MARCH, 1862

The principal water route and supply line for McClellan's proposed offensive was the James River. The Confederacy did not have much of a navy, but it did have the *Virginia*, one of only three ironclad warships afloat in the world (the French and British navies had one each); and the *Virginia* was stationed in Norfolk, protecting the entrance to the James River.

When, in 1861, the Confederates captured the Norfolk navy yard, the Union navy sunk one of its biggest steam warships, the *Merrimack*, in order to keep it out of Southern hands. The Confederates raised the vessel from the sea, cut off its top decks, and mounted ten cannons in a protective housing sheathed with two-foot thick oak and four-inch thick iron. At its bow was a four-foot iron beak that could penetrate any wooden hull the ship rammed. Renamed the *Virginia*, the ironclad was slow and clumsy in handling. The Union navy, though, had no weapons that could penetrate its armor. On its first day in action, in Hampton Roads at the mouth of the James River, the *Merrimack/Virginia* sunk two Union warships and drove a third warship aground.

When Union naval commanders heard that the Confederates were building an ironclad warship, they began constructing one of their own. The *Monitor*, designed by Swedish immigrant John Ericsson, lay low in the water. A revolving iron-clad turret housed two cannon. Towed from New York by navy tugboats, the *Monitor* had reached Chesapeake Bay when the *Merrimack/Virginia* had its first day of triumph. The next day, March 9, 1862 the two ironclads met in combat. Both ships were hit hard, but managed to stay afloat. However, with the *Monitor* stationed at the mouth of James Bay, the Confederate ironclad could do no more damage, though it did keep the federal fleet from transporting troops up the James River towards Richmond.

On May 10, 1862, Union troops recaptured Norfolk, but not before the Confederates burned their ironclad to prevent its seizure. Throughout the war, a handful of Confederate ironclads gave the Union navy problems in enforcing its blockade, but there were never enough of them, and they were too cumbersome to maneuver, to break the blockade. The Confederacy contracted with England for a fleet of ironclad rams, but Union diplomacy, and threats of war, stopped England from ever delivering them to the Confederate navy.

McClellan began his Peninsular Campaign in early April. On April 5, he laid siege to Yorktown, which was defended by a small Confederate detachment, and captured it a month later. From there, he set up a base camp near White House, Virginia, 20 miles east of Richmond. Though the Army of Potomac outnumbered General Robert E. Lee's defenders of Richmond by 110,000 to 60,000, the ever-cautious McClellan refused to attack. Instead, he waited for reinforcements from the 50,000 man corps assigned to General McDowell for the protection of Washington.

Lee understood that Richmond could not be defended against a frontal onslaught. What he needed to do was to keep McClellan diverted by going on the offensive in nearby areas. In anticipation of McClellan's offensive, in late March Lee sent Stonewall Jackson with 18,000 troops into the Shenandoah Valley where, protected by mountains on both sides, he could threaten Washington without having to commit his troops to a full-scale battle. For more than a month. Jackson mounted a brilliant campaign that tied down a much larger Union force, and ultimately compelled McClellan to send McDowell to rush troops into the Shenandoah Valley

General Stonewall Jackson

Fair Oaks reinforced McClellan's sense of caution, and instead of moving towards Richmond, he dug in and waited for the reinforcements he hoped that McDowell would provide. With Johnston incapacitated, Lee, who had been in Richmond advising the Confederate government, was given command of the entire Confederate army in Northern Virginia. While McClellan waited for an ideal time to restart his offensive, Lee took the initiative. In a series of battles lasting seven days, Lee tried to destroy McClellan's army.

The first engagement took place on June 26, 1862 at Mechanicsville, Virginia where Lee and his generals tried to crush McClellan's exposed left flank. The land was rough, with forest and swamp, and Stonewall Jackson' s delay in entering the battle allowed the Union forces to withstand the attack. The next day, Lee sent the combined armies of Generals Jackson, A.P. Hill, and James Longstreet, 57,000 men in all, against a smaller Union unit totaling 34,000 men dug in at Gaines' Mill. As night fell, the Confederates broke through the Union line.

McClellan turned away from Richmond and began a retreat across

instead of to the Richmond front as reinforcements. Jackson's audacity also forced McClellan to spread out his lines in order, if necessary, to come to the defense of Washington. On May 31, General Joseph E. Johnston attacked two of McClellan's stretched-out corps at Chickahominy River. The two-day battle, called Fair Oaks or Seven Pines, proved a standoff, although General Johnston was severely wounded. Casualties again were high: 8,000 Confederates killed and wounded to 6,000 for the Union.

White Oak Swamp to the James River, where a new Union navy base at Harrison's Landing offered him the possibility of escaping battle. Lee was so baffled by this move that he temporarily lost contact with the Union army, which was able to mass all of its units—some 90,000 men—in retreat towards the James. Recovering his bearings, Lee gave chase and on June 29 and 30 fought bayonet battles with McClellan's rearguard at Savage Station and Glendale in the Battle of Frayser's Farm, southeast of Richmond.

On July 1, at Malvern Hill near Harrison's Landing, McClellan stood to fight. With the Union navy dropping artillery on Lee's forces, and with its supply line intact, the Union forces were able to turn back the Confederate attackers. Lee had saved Richmond, but at a terrible cost. Of 95,481 Southerners who saw battle, 20,614 were killed, wounded, or missing. Of the 91,169 Union soldiers engaged in the fighting, 15,849 were similarly lost.

McClellan's army was still able to fight, however. Lincoln wanted him to resume the attack towards Richmond, but General Halleck, who had assumed command of all the Union forces, advised against it and ordered McClellan to regroup in Washington. After all the bloody fighting, the situation in Virginia was the same as if the Peninsular Campaign had never occurred.

Both sides suffered heavy casualties at the Battle of Fair Oaks

STALEMATE

General George McClellan's failure to come close to threatening Richmond, and the return of the Union army to its base in Washington, undermined public support for the war effort. After more than a year of fighting, the Union had nothing to show for its heavy casualties except the victories in the West. Even these victories were being compromised by the reluctance of the Union generals to actively pursue and fight the Confederate army.

Before coming to Washington to take command of the Union war effort, General Halleck had called a halt to the successful offensive in the West and scattered his army to occupy the border states. This allowed the Confederate Army of Tennessee, commanded by General Braxton Bragg, to pick apart isolated and undermanned Union garrisons. Bragg first moved against and defeated the Union outpost in the Cumberland Gap in the mountains separating Virginia from Tennessee. He then moved north, unimpeded, towards the Ohio River.

With Congressional elections scheduled in the North in November 1862, public support was of increasing importance. On the Republican side, Lincoln

GENERAL BRAXTON BRAGG

faced opposition from congressional radicals who wanted him to free the slaves and push the war into the South. The Democrats were also critical of Lincoln's leadership, and a faction within the party, the so-called "Copperhead Democrats," were actively sympathetic to the Southern cause and were demanding a negotiated settlement that would leave slavery untouched.

The international situation favored the Confederate side as well. Both France and Great Britain were under monarchist rule. Aristocrats in both countries were wary of the democratic Union with its call for free men and free soil. An alliance with an independent Confederacy would allow France, Britain, and other European powers to regain their influence in the New World. The Confederate need for free trade, in order to sell their cotton and tobacco exports on the European market, meshed with the need of the European industrialists to sell their manufactured goods on a global market. Europe would buy Confederate cotton in exchange for European manufactured products. The North, with its desire to protect its own industry with a protective tariff, would be isolated and undermined by a free trading European-Confederate alliance.

Great Britain almost recognized the Confederacy at the start of the war. In November 1861, Captain Charles Wilkes aboard the U.S.S. *San Jacinto* stopped and searched a British steamship, the *Trent* in international waters near the Bahamas. Two of the passengers on the *Trent*, James M. Mason and John Slidell, were Confederate diplomats en route to Great Britain to represent Southern inter-

Congressman Clement Vallandigham was the leader of the Copperheads

James Mason

ests abroad. Wilkes arrested them and brought them to Boston, where they were imprisoned in Fort Warren. The British were outraged that American naval personnel had boarded one of their vessels and arrested diplomats traveling legally.

Britain responded by sending 11,000 troops to Canada and putting the royal navy on a war footing. Although there was as much sentiment in the North to fight the British as there was in Britain to fight the North, Lincoln realized that he had to focus on the Southern rebellion and not get embroiled in a second war. With the British fleet nearing the U.S. coast, Lincoln released the prisoners and apologized to the British government. War was averted, but tensions remained.

NAPOLEON III

The success of the Confederate army in Virginia encouraged the British government to begin internal discussions about recognizing the independence of the Confederate States of America. Other European countries were also looking to undermine the Union's power. In the fall of 1862, Emperor Napoleon III of France, whose real interest was in establishing a French puppet-state in Mexico, held discussions with Southern representatives, and then talked to the governments of England and Russia, about calling for a six-month armistice. Should the Union refuse, and insist on continuing its effort to suppress the Southern rebellion, the European powers would be justified in recognizing Confederate independence. In their strategy to encourage the Confederacy, the European governments were restrained by the popular opposition within their countries to slavery. The working people of England were especially vocal in their abolitionist sentiments.

Confederate leaders understood the importance of European support for their cause. All that was needed to tip the balance towards European recognition, they believed, was further evidence of Union weakness. A successful Confederate effort to take the war to the North would damage Northern public morale and provide encouragement for European recognition. For Lee, this was the opportune time to go for a Confederate victory. He knew that neither McClellan of the Army of the Potomac nor Halleck, the commander of all the Union forces, would want to fight until they had reorganized and reinforced the Union army. Lee also understood that so strengthened, the Army of the Potomac would have the size and strength to again think about attacking Richmond. Lee proposed to take the fight to the Union and attack its forces before their generals could mount another offensive.

General Nathaniel Banks leads Union troops at the Battle of Cedar Mountain

In August 1862, General Lee sent Stonewall Jackson back into the Shenandoah Valley in order to distract the Union forces around Washington. On August 9, Jackson defeated a Union detachment led by General Nathaniel Banks at Cedar Mountain, near Culpepper, Virginia. General Halleck brought General John Pope from the West to defend Washington and stop Jackson. The Confederate cavalry greeted Pope by raiding his headquarters while he was out and stealing $350,000, Pope's dress coat, and papers that described his armies' deployment. Moving fast to confront Pope's army, Jackson marched his troops out of the mountains to Manassas Junction and destroyed a large Union storage depot. The two armies met at the Battle of Groveton on August 28-29 and it was a standoff.

Meanwhile, unsuspected by Pope, Major General James Longstreet moved his army out of the Shenandoah Valley and waited in reserve hoping Pope would renew the battle. On August 30, Pope attacked Jackson's position. Longstreet held his troops in check until all the Union forces were engaged in the battle. Then, with a rebel yell that one witness described as "like demons emerging from the earth," his army attacked. Only a stout defense by individual federal regiments allowed Pope to pull his decimated army back to Washington. The Union took 15,000 casualties, the Confederacy, 9,000. The second Battle of Manassas (or Bull Run) was, like the first battle, a decisive Confederate victory.

Lee was poised to keep up the pressure. Leaving a detachment to defend Richmond, he led his Army of Northern Virginia north, planning to destroy railroad bridges in Maryland and, hopefully, incite a popular rebellion. His likely goal was to move into Pennsylvania and destroy an important railroad bridge over the Susquehanna River in Harrisburg. This would isolate Washington from the West. It would also encourage the European countries to recognize the Confederate States of America.

MAJOR GENERAL JAMES LONGSTREET

In September, McClellan, commanding the Army of the Potomac, moved to stop Lee's invasion of Maryland. Again, however, he was too cautious and did not engage Lee's forces in a battle. Jackson, meanwhile, drove from his Shenandoah bastion and captured Harper's Ferry, with its 1,100- man Union garrison and a huge amount of military arms and ammunition. This was the high-water mark of the Confederate offensive.

Marching through Maryland, Lee found that the independent farmers in the mountains had no interest in slavery or the Southern aristocracy. It was harvest time, and they were more interested in harvesting their crops than joining the Southern rebellion. They didn't rise to greet the Confederate army. In fact, Lee lost men—more Southern soldiers deserted during the Maryland campaign than Marylanders who joined his army.

On September 12, while resting in a field near Frederick, Maryland in which Lee's army had recently camped, two Union soldiers found a package containing three cigars wrapped in paper with writing on it. The paper was titled "Headquarters, Army of Northern Virginia" and labeled "Special Orders Number 191;" it was addressed to all the generals in the Confederate army. What the Union soldiers found, and what General McClellan would soon have a copy of, was General Lee's strategic plan for the invasion of the North.

THE BRIDGE AT ANTIETAM CREEK

For the moment, at least, Lee's army was scattered, waiting for Jackson to leave Harper's Ferry and open the way for both armies to unite as a powerful invasion force in Hagerstown, Maryland. If McClellan used the information dropped into his lap and moved fast, he could bring his entire army against Lee's isolated forces and defeat them one at a time. However, McClellan was not a general who believed in hasty movements. His orders to his commanders gave no hint that a rapid deployment and quick attack could defeat the Confederate army and perhaps even end the war.

With his customary caution, McClellan sent his army of 70,000 men through Crampton's Gap and captured South Mountain. Then instead of carrying the battle to the out-numbered Confederates below, he stopped to survey the situation. This gave Stonewall Jackson time to recross the Potomac and come to Lee's aid below South Mountain. Still, the Confederate forces were outnumbered two to one, and were camped at the little hamlet of Sharpsburg, Maryland, along Antietam Creek, with their backs against the Potomac River and no way to maneuver.

On September 17, 1862, the two armies collided. McClellan's forces attacked the Confederate left flank, which Lee desperately reinforced. The fighting spread to the center of the battlefield, which came to be called Bloody Lane, so-named because of the fierce hand-to-hand fighting between the two sides. Union troops led by General Ambrose Burnside nearly

President Lincoln meets with General McClellan and his staff

broke through on the Confederate right, and were set to attack Sharpsburg, but were repulsed by cavalry under General A.P. Hill.

By nightfall the fighting had ended; Lee's lines had held, but the Battle of Antietam was the bloodiest battle of the war. The Confederates had 2,700 men killed and 9,029 wounded; Union casualties were 2,108 dead and 9,549 wounded. The next day Lee withdrew his forces back across the Potomac into Virginia. Had McClellan called in available reinforcements and pursued Lee's broken army, he could have destroyed it right there. McClellan considered Lee's retreat from Maryland a victory, however, and basked in that glory without continuing the fight.

Two weeks later, the Confederate offensive in the West was stopped cold at a battle in Perryville, Kentucky. The Confederate Army of Tennessee under General Braxton Bragg was racing ahead of the Union army, under Major General Don Carlos Buell, hoping to cross the Ohio River and bring the war into Ohio. Bragg's army was carrying equipment to supply new recruits that the Confederates expected to be flocking to their lines. However, Kentuckians remained faithful to the Union and did not join up. Precious time was wasted in an effort to install a secessionist government in Kentucky's capital of

Frankfort; it collapsed as soon as Bragg's army left.

Meanwhile, Buell was able to make time and, on October 8, he blocked Bragg's march north towards Ohio. The battle of Perryville was a standoff, but Bragg decided to retreat back to Tennessee. Buell, typical of Union commanders, did not go after him. Further west, however, Grant's army had cleared Confederate troops out of Northern Mississippi and was planning an overland siege of Vicksburg, the last Confederate outpost on the Mississippi River.

General Ambrose Burnside

In the East, General McClellan had let six weeks pass before he crossed the Potomac and resumed the offensive; even then, he continued his slow, deliberate pace. In the interim, a Confederate cavalry, led by Brigadier General J.E.B. Stuart, made a dashing raid inside Pennsylvania. Stuart's invasion, from October 8 to October 10, had little military significance. Still, that a Confederate cavalry could so easily get around the much larger Union forces was another blow to Northern morale. Lincoln finally ran out of patience; on November 7, he fired McClellan. His replacement, General Ambrose Burnside, had more vigor, but less competence. This would soon become glaringly obvious in the Union debacle at Fredericksburg, Virginia.

The year 1862 ended with Lee still in command of the routes towards Richmond. However, the Confederate plan to invade the North, Stuart's raid notwithstanding, had been beaten back in Kentucky and Maryland. The South's failure to bring the war to the North had discouraged Great Britain and the other European countries from recognizing the Confederate States of America as an independent country. At the same time, President Lincoln was about to take a bold step that would alter the context of the war—and establish a principle that changed the course of American history.

EMANCIPATION

Though Abraham Lincoln was not an abolitionist, he had always considered slavery to be immoral, and in his political speeches he had always made that point. In his senate campaign against Stephen Douglas in 1858, he had come out against racism as well as slavery, saying, "Let us discard all this quibbling about this man and the other man—this race and that race and the other race being inferior, and therefore they must be placed in an inferior position. Let us discard all these things, and unite as one people throughout the land, until we shall once more stand up declaring that all men are created equal."

Lincoln's position on race put him far ahead of popular opinion, however. In the South, slaves were considered property; they had no individual rights or freedoms. There were some free blacks living in the South—slaves who had been given their freedom by their owners—but they had few basic rights. And while slavery was legally prohibited in the Northern states, free black people were still very much second-class citizens. Only the New England states of Maine, New Hampshire, Vermont, and Massachusetts allowed black males to vote; no states allowed blacks to hold legal authority over whites. Blacks could not serve on juries or, practically speaking, win election to public office. Ohio, Indiana, Oregon, and even Lincoln's own state of Illinois, had laws aimed at discouraging free blacks from settling within their borders.

Though Lincoln did not believe that the United States could exist as "half slave and half free," he disagreed with the abolitionist's determination to free the slaves no matter what the consequence. Instead, Lincoln hoped—naively it turned out—that economic reality would end the institution. However, Northern opposition to slavery only strengthened slavery's hold on the Southern mind. The Confederacy was founded on the idea of preserving slavery even though some of its leaders, Robert E. Lee among them, had freed their own slaves and were opposed to the institution.

By mid-1862, with the war in the East at a stalemate, and with England, France and other foreign powers threatening to recognize the Confederate States of

America, Lincoln believed that he had to do something to build popular enthusiasm for the war. He had long considered freeing the slaves, but felt that he must have the support of public opinion to do so. An antislavery stand must unite Northerners in a moral crusade, not divide them under the banner of racism. Lincoln could not frame emancipation as a desperate move; he had to link it to battlefield progress, a military victory. Abolitionists were still a small political minority, and racism, even in the North, was the natural state.

The Battle of Antietam gave Lincoln the context he needed to move against slavery. At Antietam, the Confederate invasion of the North was turned back. Though overly cautious military leadership prevented the Union from winning a resounding victory, the seemingly invincible General Lee was forced back to the protection of Richmond and the defense of Southern soil.

Lincoln had first raised the idea of freeing the slaves at a cabinet meeting on July 22. Opposition from within his cabinet encouraged him to drop the idea. Then on September 22, 1862, five days after Antietam, Lincoln issued a preliminary Emancipation Proclamation, informing his cabinet that he would tolerate no dissenters. The proclamation stated that on January 1, 1863 all slaves held in a state that was in rebellion against the federal government would be "then, thenceforward and forever free."

Abraham Lincoln

However bold the proclamation sounded, it didn't have any legal authority to free any slaves. By limiting emancipation to only those areas that were still in rebellion—that is, still part of the Confederacy—Lincoln allowed himself no authority, other than military victory, to enforce the proclamation. Moreover, the proclamation did nothing to change the property status of those slaves living in the border states, or in any part of the South that was already under federal authority and, hence, no longer in rebellion. In these areas, Lincoln promoted the idea of voluntary emancipation for which former slaveholders would receive compensation.

In addition, Lincoln issued the proclamation without consulting Congress. His justification was that the Emancipation Proclamation was a war measure and, that as commander-in-chief, he was empowered to take any measure to win the war. Wanting to assure it's legality, however, Lincoln advocated a constitutional amendment that would prohibit slavery everywhere. (Congress eventually passed, and the required three-fourths

PRESIDENT LINCOLN READS THE EMANCIPATION PROCLAMATION TO HIS CABINET

The Emancipation Proclamation was not well received in the North. Radical Republican abolitionists thought Lincoln was too cautious; they wanted him to abolish slavery everywhere. Other people objected to the whole idea of unilateral emancipation. Where would the freed slaves go? Many working people feared that they would flee to the North and compete with them for factory jobs. The slaves themselves understood the emancipation as an act that

number of states ratified, just such a measure. The 13th Amendment became part of the Constitution in 1865.)

PLANTATION SLAVES FREED BY UNION FORCES

transformed the Civil War into their own liberation struggle.

In the elections of 1862, the Democrats gained 35 congressional seats, control of 3 state legislatures and the governorships of New York and New Jersey. The Democrats out-polled Republicans in the midwestern states, including Lincoln's home state of Illinois. Lincoln described himself as "like the boy who stubbed his toe on the way to see his girl; he was too big to cry, and it hurt too much to laugh." Republicans, however, still controlled both the Senate and the House. New England and the newly-settled West, where the principle of free soil was strongly favored, were Republican strongholds. Republicans also did better than expected in the border states, and this was a key to their majority. Lincoln was now in control. With the election behind him, he was free of having to appease the Democrats, and he could rid the army of General McClellan, who was a Democratic favorite.

The Emancipation Proclamation had its most immediate effect on England, France and other European countries where slavery had never taken root. The proclamation put an end to the possibility that European nations would recognize the Confederacy. Antislavey sentiment was popular in Europe, especially in England where, after the Emancipation, working people held rallies in support of the Union. Lincoln's proclamation, in effect, isolated the South. Europe might recognize the Confederacy in terms of challenging the Union as a political institution and economic power, but it could not recognize the Confederacy as a bastion of slave labor.

AN ALL BLACK REGIMENT IN THE UNION ARMY, THE 107TH U.S. COLORED INFANTRY

The domestic impact of the Emancipation Proclamation was most directly felt by the Union army. When the Union forces marched South, they often came upon large plantations. As slave labor, the blacks were assets to the Confederate cause, producing the food and the export crops necessary to sustain the Confederacy. In Tennessee, Northern Alabama, and Mississippi, Union forces burned crops, barns, and plantation houses, tore up rail lines, and destroyed factories. Many plantation owners, fleeing the army, tried to take their slaves with them. Yet the very act of abandoning their plantations shattered the authority by which they could hold them. Wherever the Union army went, they were followed by slaves who assumed that they were free.

The Union commanders didn't know what to do with these followers. Initially, the ex-slaves were left to fend for themselves. However, as their numbers grew, the army took on the challenge of building camps for them and feeding them. Then they started using them to build roads and fortifications. The refugee camps needed police to keep order, which few white soldiers were willing to do. So the army began recruiting the ex-slaves to police the camps. It wasn't long before the army realized that the blacks would make good soldiers, enthusiastic about fighting the Confederates and liberating other slaves in the process. By the middle of 1863, black regiments, commanded by white officers, were being organized by the Union army; ultimately, 150,000 former slaves would don the blue Union army uniform and take part in the war.

Most of the black regiments were limited to guard duty, or the performance of physical labor that white soldiers did not want to do. Those units that saw combat duty performed heroically, however. This created a new situation for the ex-slaves. How could the North deny citizen status to blacks who fought for the Union? And if some ex-slaves were to be granted citizen status, how could others be denied that right?

MAJOR MARTIN DELANY WAS THE FIRST BLACK UNION OFFICER IN THE CIVIL WAR

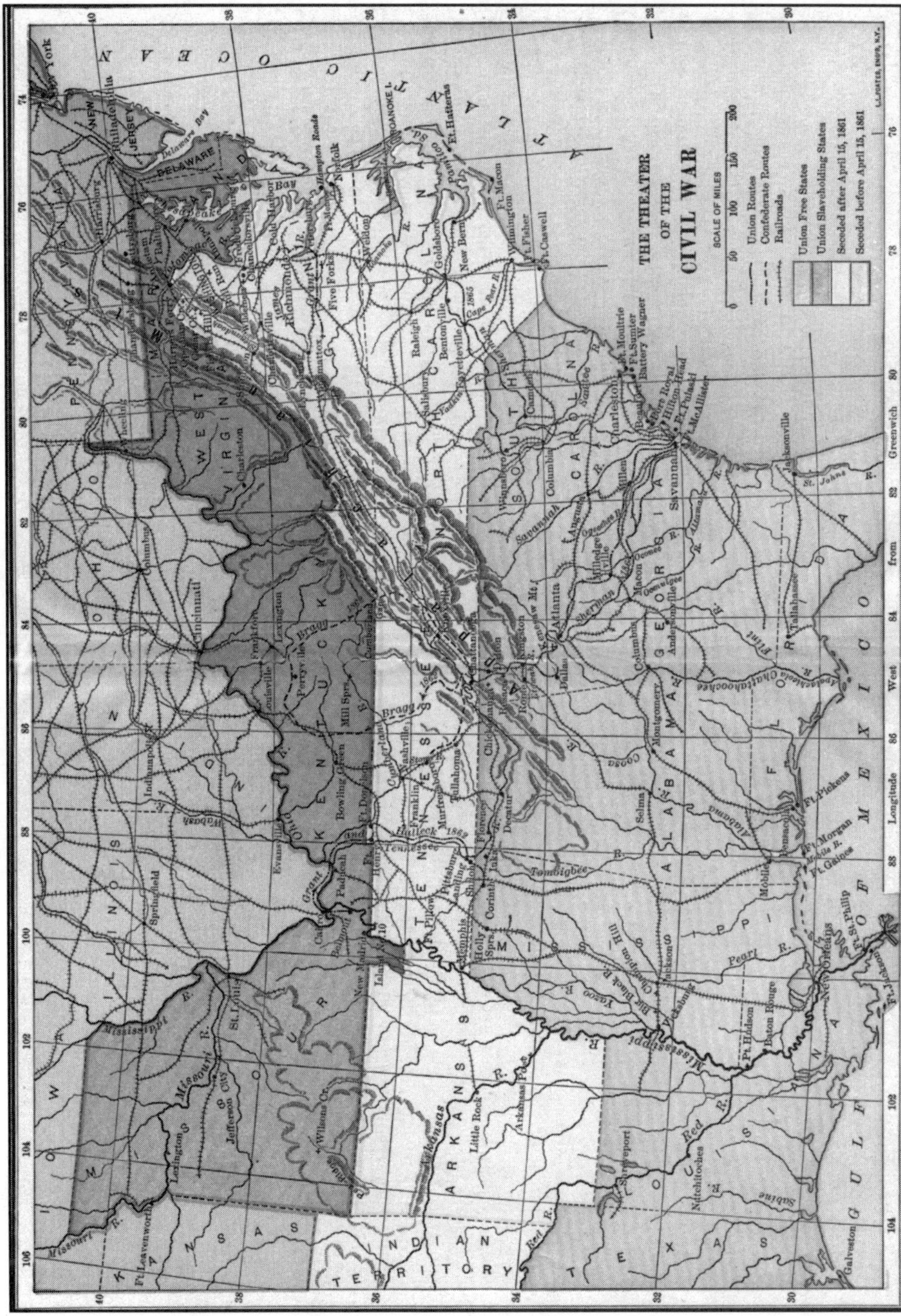

The Theater of the Civil War

THE WAR EFFORT, NORTH AND SOUTH

No one, North or South, had anticipated that the war would last very long, or that there would thousands of casualties. Most Northerners, including Lincoln, believed that a few defeats would cause the South to capitulate. However, in the battles between the Army of the Potomac and the Army of Northern Virginia, on which public attention was most focused, the Confederacy was the consistent victor. This led to a brief period of Confederate overconfidence. After the first Battle of Bull Run, Southerners had disdain for the North's ability to fight, and exaggerated their own military prowess. Over time, though, Lincoln, Lee, and other knowledgeable leaders on both sides realized that it would be a long and bloody war; they also realized they would have to build and hold public support for their war efforts, and find a way to recruit more soldiers.

It was not just the shocking numbers of men killed in battle that made recruitment so necessary. Medical science was still nearly primitive. Doctors knew nothing about sanitation, sterilization, infections, or what caused sickness and disease. Despite the efforts of nurses such as Clara Barton, who would later start the American Red Cross, and Sally Thompson, who organized medical care for the Confederate side, health conditions in both armies

CLARA BARTON

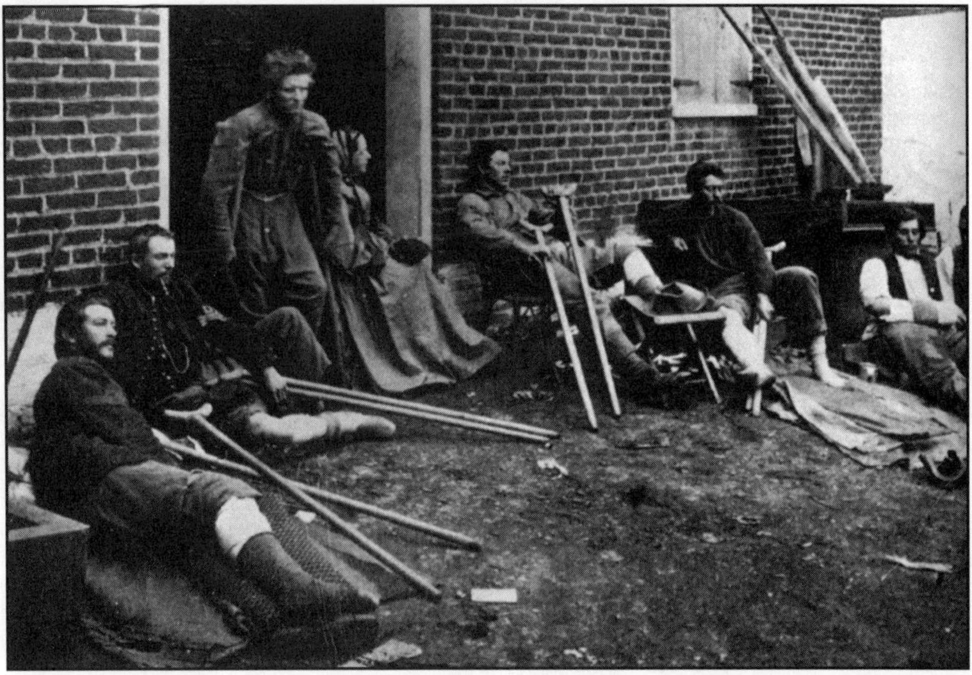

A FIELD HOSPITAL AT FREDERICKSBURG, VIRGINIA

were abominable. No one knew about protecting or purifying drinking water. In camp, soldiers suffered from dysentery, typhoid, and pneumonia. It was estimated that for every Confederate soldier killed in battle, three more died of disease. For the Union army, the estimate was two and one-half to one.

Wounded soldiers were as likely to die from their wounds as they were to return to battle. According to one estimate, the number of men who died of their wounds was approximately two-thirds of the number who died instantly in battle. Approximately one half of the men wounded in battle were lost to the military forever. Amputation was the most common way of treating leg and arm wounds. There were no sedatives, no pain-killers, no way of putting a man to sleep during an operation. Medics held a man down while doctors sawed through the bone and then tried to stop the wounded man from bleeding to death in the process.

At the beginning of the war, prisoner exchanges were commonplace. However, as the war dragged on and manpower became an issue, these exchanges stopped. What was the sense of returning prisoners to fight again in the other side's army? Prison camps on both sides became death pits. It wasn't so much that either side wanted to deliberately mistreat the other side's soldiers. As with battlefield conditions, there was no knowledge of sanitation and other health standards. The prisons were horribly overcrowded, the

ANDERSONVILLE PRISON

water polluted, the food terrible, and the medical care unhelpful. Out of some 220,000 Confederates held in prisons in the North, 26,426 died; for the Union, the numbers were 126,950 and 22,576 deaths.

The sheer size of the Union war machine, especially the advantage the North had in terms of population, threatened the future of the Confederacy. Despite the opposition of many Confederate states' righters, General Lee convinced Jefferson Davis to introduce a system of conscription. The Confederate Conscription Act, passed on April 16, 1862, required the service of most every white male between the ages of 18 and 35. On February 17, 1864 a new measure was passed expanding the draft age from 17 to 50. However, many skilled professions were exempted, including slave overseers, at the rate of one exemption for every 20 slaves. Draft evasion was commonplace, especially among the poor farmers who had no self-interest in defending slavery. The desertion rate of about 10 percent was also a problem, so much so that Jefferson Davis had to declare amnesties in order to persuade deserters to return to the Confederate army.

The Union, with its greater population pool, didn't resort to conscription until March 1863. The new law made all men between 20 and 45 eligible for military service, but exempted any one who could pay $300 to hire a substitute. Since $300 was a lot of money at the time, the law benefited only the wealthiest Northerners who could buy their way out of the service. As in the South, draft evasion was commonplace. In the North, many poor working people were infuriated by the legislation. When the names of the first draftees were published in New York City newspapers in July of 1863, working people went on a rampage, burning symbols of federal authority, looting, and lynching blacks who they blamed for the war. Union troops had to be sent in to suppress the so-called "anti-draft riots."

Nevertheless, support for the war remained high on both sides. Lincoln's great accomplishment was rallying the North behind the idea of preserving the Union and investing this goal with the moral crusade of human rights and free labor. Another reason why Northerners supported the war was that it led to a boom in the economy. Factories worked at full capacity in the North, supplying weapons and materials for the Union soldiers and sailors. Government contracts gave Northern industrialists the capital and the incentive to expand and utilize new technology; the number of wealthy industrialists greatly expanded thanks to war contracts and, because government over-

ANTI-DRAFT RIOTS TOOK PLACE IN NEW YORK IN 1863

DuPont factories such as these supplied the Union with gunpowder

Destroyed railroad in the South

sight was unsophisticated, war-profiteering.

The sewing-machine allowed industrialists to step up production of clothing. The mechanical reaper and other new agricultural implements made farming easier and more productive. Farmers had a ready market for their produce in the U.S. government, and also benefited by poor European grain crops. Eight hundred thousand immigrants settled in the North during the Civil War and found work in factories and farms. Wages, however, which rose 43 percent during the war, did not keep up with the 117 percent rise in prices.

In contrast, the war had a negative effect on the Confederate economy. Most of the war was fought in Southern territory and this led to the destruction of the Southern infrastructure, especially the railroads. Because of a lack of manpower, women had to step forward to run the farms and plantations, which they did until the emancipation of the slaves brought about a crisis in Southern farm labor. Without any industrial base to begin with, the South had to pour all of its industrial resources into starting up manufacturing plants for war material. The Union's naval blockade, though not completely successful, diminished the export of cotton and other export staples.

However, to many Southerners, the Confederate cause had a religious dimension. Many of them believed that God was on their side, that slavery reflected the natural moral order. Southern churches, almost all of which were Protestant, enthusiastically supported the war effort. Confederate defeats were marked in these churches by "fasting, humiliation, and prayer." Confederate Vice President Stephens accurately described the mood of civilians when he wrote in early 1863, that "the great majority of the masses both North and South are true to the cause of their side. . . A large majority on both sides is tired of the war; want peace. . . . But as we do not want peace without independence, so they do not want peace without union." And so the war continued.

ALEXANDER STEPHENS

THE TURNING OF THE TIDE

By issuing the Emancipation Proclamation, Lincoln had transformed the moral basis for the Civil War; however, he was still not able to find a general to match the skill of the Confederate army's Robert E. Lee. After the victory at Antietam, with the Confederate army shattered, Lincoln ordered General McClellan to "cross the Potomac and give battle to the enemy, or drive him South." McClellan again procrastinated, and on November 7, 1862 Lincoln replaced him with Major General Ambrose E. Burnside.

A West Point graduate, Burnside had enthusiasm, but not much military skill. He set out towards Richmond with an army of 123,000, and was in a position

President Lincoln discusses strategy with General McClellan

UNION FORCES CROSS THE RAPPAHANNOCK ON PONTOON BRIDGES

to move on the Confederate capital before General Lee was in a position to stop him. However, Burnside too, procrastinated, wasting almost three weeks camped with his army along the banks of the Rappahannock River across from Fredericksburg, Virginia.

Fredericksburg was lightly defended, and a quick crossing would have given Burnside an opportunity to march unimpeded into Richmond. However, a November storm had made the river high. Rather then risk a dangerous crossing, Burnside sat tight waiting for pontoon bridges to arrive. This gave Stonewall Jackson time to rush his troops from the Shenandoah Valley to Fredericksburg, and time for Lee to place his 77,000 men in an impregnable defensive position on Marye's Heights overlooking the town.

THE UNION ARMY SUFFERED HEAVY CASUALTIES AT MARYE'S HEIGHTS

Rather than change his plan and try to move around the newly strengthened Confederate position, Burnside crossed the river and, on December 13, ordered a frontal assault. Many of the Union soldiers understood the futility of the attack, but nevertheless followed their commanders' orders. One enlisted man, asked by a reporter what the Confederates on Marye's Heights were up to, replied, "They want us to get in. Getting out won't be quite so smart and easy."

Six times Burnside's Army of the Potomac moved forward across an open field under Marye's Heights. Advancing in long, orderly double lines with battle flags flying, they were sitting ducks for the Confederate artillery taking aim at them from above. Nine thousand Union soldiers were killed or wounded during this one assault. The Confederate defenders at the top of the hill lost 1,500. The next day, Burnside pulled his battered army back across the Rappahannock. Overall, Fredericksburg cost the Army of the Potomac 12,700 men; the Confederates lost 5,400.

Major General Joseph Hooker

Once again, Richmond was saved and the Union Army of the Potomac was defeated and in retreat. Lincoln, horrified by the casualties, fired Burnside and replaced him with Major General "Fighting Joe" Hooker, but the demoralized and shattered Army of the Potomac was finished fighting for the year.

The war was going better for the Union in the West. By the winter of 1862, the combined Union army and navy had cleared the Mississippi River of all Confederate outposts except those guarding the high bluffs on the eastern shore between Port Hudson, Louisiana, and Vicksburg, Mississippi. It was between these two fortresses that supplies from the West were able to enter the Confederacy. If the Union could capture these strongholds, it would have complete control of the Mississippi River and sever the connection between the deep South and the Confederate states west of the Mississippi—Louisiana, Arkansas, and Texas.

The Confederate artillery, positioned on the bluffs overlooking the river at Vicksburg, was impregnable by frontal assault. So in December 1862, General Grant, commander of the Army of Tennessee, tried to outflank the Southerners by approaching Vicksburg from the north. However, his army got bogged down in the swampy woodland around the Yazoo River and could not find a way to mount an attack. Still, the difficulty didn't deter Grant from moving forward. He simply came up with a different and even bolder plan. He decided to approach Vicksburg from the south, advancing through Confederate territory, and living in large part off the land.

ADMIRAL DAVID PORTER

In April 1863, Grant crossed over to the west bank of the Mississippi River and marched 20 miles south past Vicksburg to Grand Gulf, where there was an easy crossing back into Mississippi. His march was coordinated with a naval armada led by Rear Admiral David D. Porter. On the night of April 16, his fleet shut down its lights and engines and tried to float silently downriver past the Vicksburg batteries. It was discovered, and the Confederates unleashed an artillery barrage. Only one Union ship was hit, however; the rest floated safely past the fortress and met up with Grant at Grand Gulf.

Grant crossed the river with 20,000 men and began to march east in an attempt to outflank Lieutenant General John C. Pemberton who, with 30,000 men, was protecting Vicksburg. Without a supply line, Grant won five small but pitched battles against Southern troops sent out to stop him. Grant's army also captured 8,000 Confederate soldiers in the process.

A Confederate army of 20,000 men, led by General Joe Johnston, started out from Chattanooga, Tennessee in order to intercept Grant before he could begin his attack on Vicksburg. Anticipating Johnston's route, Grant seized the railroad junction at Jackson, Mississippi and delayed Johnston's mission.

Utilizing former slaves to help move his army—thus freeing his own men from the labors of breaking and setting up nightly encampments—Grant was able to outflank Pemberton's forces and force them back into Vicksburg. By mid-May, Grant's Army of Tennessee had grown, with reinforcements, to 75,000 men, enough to effectively surround the city in an arc spreading from the north to the east and around to the south. With the Union navy in control of the Mississippi River, the Confederates defending Vicksburg had no way to escape.

On May 19, Grant tried a frontal attack, but the Confederate defenders beat it back. Rather than take more casualties, Grant simply laid siege and waited for Pemberton and his men to run out of food. On July 4, 1863 Pemberton surrendered his army. Instead of transporting the Confederates to a Northern prison camp, Grant allowed the soldiers to go back home. Rather than take prisoners-of-war who would further strain the resources of the North, Grant preferred that the defeated men become a burden to the South.

LIEUTENANT JOHN C. PEMBERTON

Five days after the capture of Vicksburg, Port Hudson, the last Confederate stronghold on the Mississippi, fell to a small Union army led by General Nathaniel Banks. Like Grant, Banks freed slaves as he marched north out of New Orleans and employed them in his army. The Mississippi River, from New Orleans north, was now controlled by Union forces. An attempt by General Joseph Johnston to recapture Vicksburg was stopped by Major General William Tecumseh Sherman, whose forces then entered Jackson, Mississippi and burned it.

While Grant was winning in the West, General Lee continued to frustrate the Army of the Potomac in the East. After a winter of restoring the army's strength and morale, General Hooker once more set out to capture Richmond, assuring Lincoln, "May God have mercy on General Lee, for I will have none." With more than 120,000 men, double the number that Lee had available for his Army of Northern Virginia, Hooker was confident of victory—perhaps, as Lincoln worried, too confident.

Hooker's plan was to keep one part of his army to hold Lee's attention in Fredericksburg, while he moved the larger part through a heavily wooded area called the Wilderness around Lee's flank so he could be in position, near Chancellorsville, to attack the Army of Northern Virginia from the rear.

Lee, however, tracked Hooker's movements and anticipated his plan. He first sent his cavalry, led by Jeb Stuart, towards Chancellorsville in order to distract and confuse Hooker's army. Instead

General Joe Hooker at Chancellorsville

of continuing the advance, Hooker reacted to Stuart's feint by setting up a defensive position. Lee again split his forces. One detachment remained in Fredericksburg in order to keep the Union troops, opposite them, from going to Hooker's aid. Lee himself led 50,000 soldiers to attack Hooker at Chancellorsville. Seeing Hooker in a defensive position, he sent Stonewall Jackson, in command of 26,000 troops, to swing around Hooker's army so he could it attack on its right flank, where Hooker's superiority in numbers would not be overwhelming.

On May 2, 1863, Jackson's troops attacked the Army of the Potomac's XI Corps that was defending Hooker's flank and routed it. Jackson then turned on the center of the Union line, commanded by Major General Daniel Sickles, and sent it reeling. Despite these defeats, Hooker's army still outnumbered Lee by two to one. Hooker, however, had lost all confidence in himself and went on the defensive. A large portion of the Army of the Potomac was never ordered into battle.

While the Battle of Chancellorsville was going on, Union Major General John Sedgwick stormed Marye's Heights in Fredericksburg and overwhelmed a much smaller Confederate unit commanded by Lieutenant General Jubal Early. Flush with victory, Sedgwick then set out to help Hooker at Chancellorsville. Certain that Hooker would not resume his attack, Lee detached part of his army and stopped

Sedgwick's advance at Salem's Church, five miles from Chancellorsville. Totally demoralized, on May 5 Hooker ordered a retreat back across the Rappahannock. The Army of the Potomac lost 17,000 men at Chancellorsville, the Army of Northern Virginia, about 11,000. However, one of those was Stonewall Jackson, who was shot by his own men during the attack on May 2 in the confusion of the battle. Jackson died on May 10, depriving Lee of his ablest general; "my right arm," Lee called him.

After Chancellorsville, Lee had the choice of sending part of his army west to bolster the forces fighting Grant near Vicksburg, or to duplicate what Grant was doing in Mississippi—take the war to enemy territory and destroy areas of Maryland and Pennsylvania. Though the Confederates lacked the resources to sustain an invasion of the North, Lee and Jefferson Davis hoped that a successful foray might demoralize Union supporters. Indeed, as Lee moved North, Confederate Vice President Alexander Stephens prepared to travel to Washington under a flag of truce to negotiate the South's independence. The Confederates hoped that, with the Army of the Potomac again defeated, Lincoln would be willing to negotiate an end to the war. However, the Confederates underestimated the president. Unwilling to consider any terms short of the South's return to the Union, Lincoln refused to even meet with the Confederate emissary.

Despite Lee's string of successes, the war was wearing the South down. The North had the manpower to keep filling the ranks of the Army of the Potomac;

THE BATTLE OF CHANCELLORSVILLE

the South was at a point where it could not sustain its manpower loses and continue fighting. An invasion of Pennsylvania was a long shot. In retrospect, it was the Confederacy's last hope of victory.

Leaving one corps to protect Richmond, Lee started to move his army northward on June 3, sending Lieutenant General Richard S. Ewell to clear the Shenandoah Valley of Union forces, which he quickly did. General Hooker saw the division of Lee's forces as an opportunity to again attack Richmond. However, Lincoln, who no longer trusted Hooker's ability, but could not then fire him because of Hooker's political support, told him that "Lee's army, and not Richmond, is your true objective point."

The Army of Northern Virginia followed Ewell through the Great Valley, and by June 27 the entire army had crossed the Potomac and was marching through Maryland into Pennsylvania. The next day, Confederate General Jubal Early held the city of York, 20 miles south of the capital at Harrisburg, hostage, demanding as its ransom, boots and money. Hooker's Army of the Potomac shadowed Lee's army north, keeping to its right—or eastern—flank in position to protect Washington should Lee decide to attack to the east.

GENERAL JUBAL A. EARLY

On June 28, General Hooker got into an argument with his superior, General Halleck, over the defense of Harper's Ferry and resigned. More likely, Hooker resented Lincoln's lack of trust in him and wanted a way out. He was quickly replaced by Major General George Gordon Meade, a professional soldier with a reputation for being steady and dependable.

On June 23, Lee sent Brigadier General Jeb

GENERAL GEORGE MEADE

Stuart's cavalry on a raid towards Washington. Lee hoped that Meade would concentrate on stopping Stuart, and thus allow Lee's main force to do damage in Pennsylvania. Meade didn't bite; Stuart's cavalry attacked a wagon train just four miles outside of Washington, but Meade kept his forces focused on Lee's army. Stuart's foray proved a hollow victory for the Confederacy, for without the cavalry scouting ahead as the "eyes" of his army, Lee momentarily lost contact with the movements of Meade's army.

Both Lee and Meade planned to position their troops in advantageous defensive positions: Lee on South Mountain near Cashtown, Pennsylvania; Meade behind Pipe Creek near Frederick, Maryland. However, on July 1 Confederate troops, which were often poorly supplied, entered the town of Gettysburg, Pennsylvania looking for extra boots. They came upon a Union cavalry division, and fierce fighting broke out. The Confederates got the better of it and drove the cavalry to Cemetery Ridge, just south of the town. For a while, the Union had only 5,000 men available to hold the position. However, with its hooked shape, the ridge was an excellent defensive position. General Meade decided to stand and fight, and reinforcements from the south and east rushed up the ridge to defend the position.

Seeing his advantage, but having no idea of where the major part of Meade's army was located, Lee hurried

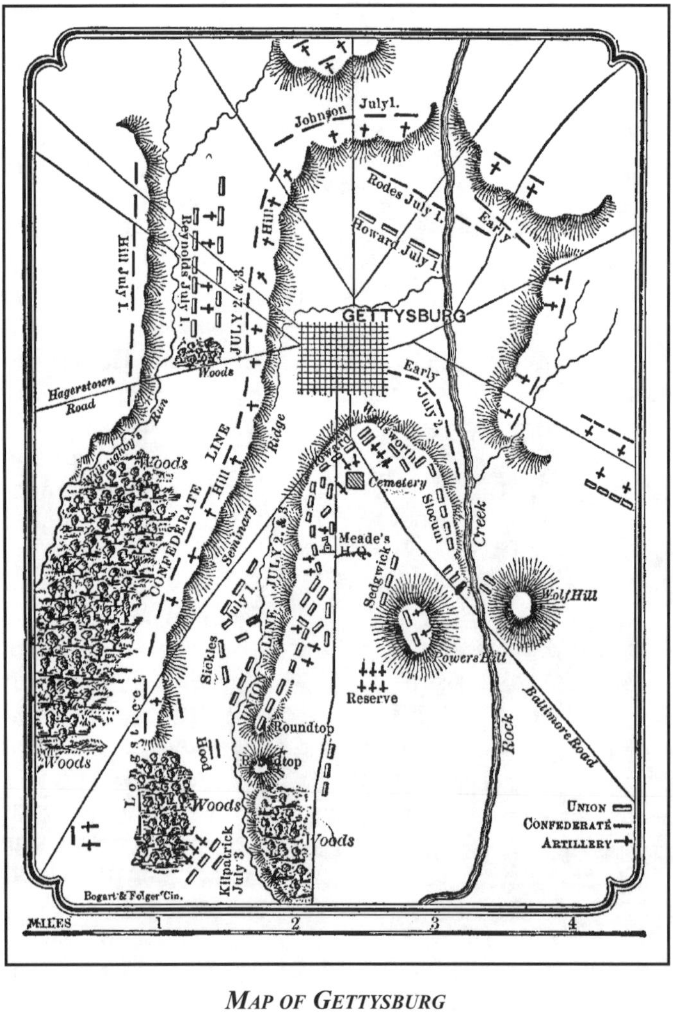

MAP OF GETTYSBURG

his troops from Cashtown towards Gettysburg, establishing a position along Seminary Ridge, across from Cemetery Ridge where the Union forces were digging in. On July 2 the Confederates attacked in force. Lieutenant General James Longstreet's troops drove the Union forces out of the peach orchard in front of Cemetery Ridge, and troops led by Lieutenant General John B. Hood almost took control of Little Round Top, a hill that would have allowed him to bombard the Union position on Cemetery Ridge. Troops from New England and New York

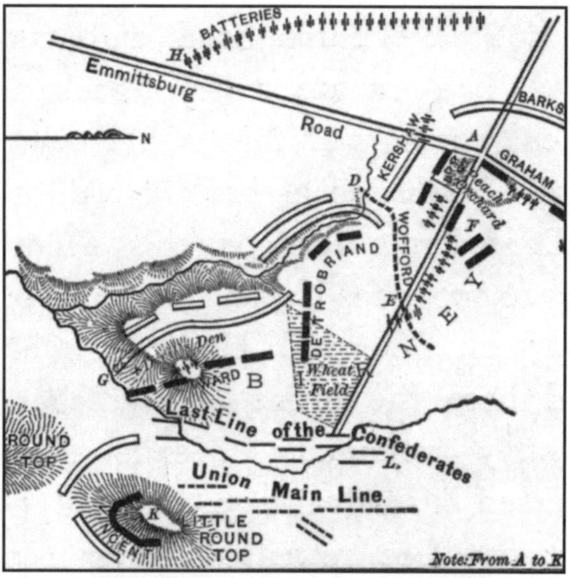

Map of Little Round Top

Confederate attack on Cemetery Ridge

PICKETT'S CHARGE

counterattacked with fixed bayonets and drove the Confederates off the hill. Generals Ewell and Early also had near successes in driving the Union troops from Cemetery Ridge. Indeed, Ewell's forces held the lower slopes of Culp's Hill overnight, but were driven back the next morning after several hours of fighting.

By the end of the second day's fighting, both flanks of the Union army had been attacked and both had held, despite losing ground. That night, in a council of war, Meade told his commanders that he believed Lee would assault the center of their line the next day; the Union leader also determined that his army would stay and fight.

After the early morning attack by the Confederates on Culp's Hill was repulsed, an eerie quiet settled on the battlefield. Meade, anticipating what Lee would do next, strengthened the center of his line on top of Cemetery Ridge. Lee, against Longstreet's advice, had decided on a frontal assault up the slopes of the ridge. It began in the early afternoon with an artillery barrage that missed its mark. Then the Southerners, 15,000 strong, attacked, "an overwhelming resistless tide of an ocean of armed men sweeping upon us," as one Union observer described it. Withering fire from the Union batteries on Little Round Top and Cemetery Ridge decimated their ranks until there was only one Confederate division left to move forward.

Led by Major General George E. Pickett, these troops charged through the Union gunfire. One group made it to the top of the ridge, but Union reinforcements kept joining the battle. Artillery fire shook the Confederate ranks with deadly accuracy as the Rebel flanks were smashed in. "Pickett's Charge" was the greatest tactical error Lee ever made. The Confederates suffered thousands of casualties in a desperate attack that gained nothing. As he viewed the debacle of his surviving troops in retreat, Lee said, "All this is my fault."

A hard rain fell the next day, July 4. The battlefield was quiet as both armies dealt with their dead and tended their wounded. In three days of fighting the Union casualties—killed, wounded, captured, or missing—came to about 23,000

DEAD SOLDIERS AT GETTYSBURG

men; the Confederate casualties were more than 28,000. Medical aid, supplies, and recruited nurses poured into Gettysburg from all over the Northeast to deal with the crisis.

On July 5, Lee turned his bloodied army south and began a retreat to Virginia. High water on the Potomac prevented an immediate crossing. Lincoln ordered Meade to attack, but Meade, who's own army was battered, delayed. Lincoln was furious that, as at Antietam, a Union general did not have the will to administer a crushing blow to Lee's Army of Northern Virginia. However, Lincoln appreciated that Meade had stopped Lee's invasion of Pennsylvania, and that the Confederacy no longer had the resources or manpower to take the war to the Union.

The victories at Vicksburg and Gettysburg also signaled to Europe that the Union could not be defeated. Shortly after Gettysburg, Confederate orders for ironclad naval vessels, under construction in France and England, were canceled by those governments. General Lee took full responsibility for the Confederate defeat at Gettysburg and tendered his resignation. Jefferson Davis rejected it, but considered Gettysburg "the darkest hour of our political existence."

The Gettysburg Address was delivered by President Lincoln on November 19, 1863 at the dedication of the national cemetery at Gettysburg, Pennsylvania.

Fourscore and seven years ago our fathers brought forth on this continent, a new nation, conceived in liberty, and dedicated to the proposition that all men are created equal.

Now we are engaged in a great civil war, testing whether that nation, or any nation so conceived and so dedicated, can long endure. We are met on a great battlefield of that war. We have come to dedicate a portion of that field, as a final resting place for those who here gave their lives that that nation might live. It is altogether fitting and proper that we should do this.

But in a larger sense, we can not dedicate—we can not consecrate—we can not hallow—this ground. The brave men, living and dead, who struggled here have consecrated it, far above our poor power to add or detract. The world will little note, nor long remember, what we say here, but it can never forget what they did here. It is for us, the living, rather to be dedicated here to the unfinished work which they who fought here have thus far so nobly advanced. It is rather for us to be here dedicated to the great task remaining before us, that from these honored dead we take increased devotion to that cause for which they gave the last full measure of devotion; that we here highly resolve that these dead shall not have died in vain; that this nation, under God, shall have a new birth of freedom, and that this government of the people, by the people, for the people, shall not perish from the earth.

Even in victory, the North was stunned by the carnage at Gettysburg, and the difficulty of dealing with the wounded of both sides and burying their dead. Pennsylvania's Governor, Andrew Curtin, commissioned a local attorney to purchase land for a proper burial ground for Union dead. A 17-acre site on Cemetery Hill was designated as a military cemetery, and on November 19, President Lincoln took a train to Gettysburg for the dedication ceremony.

The principal speaker was Edward Everett, a well-known orator and political leader. Everett spoke for two hours, in a well-received speech whose words are now forgotten. He was followed by President Lincoln, who had been asked only to make "a few appropriate remarks" for the occasion. Lincoln's address consisted of ten sentences, just 272 words. He thought his speech a failure, but Everett told him that "I should be glad if I could flatter myself that I came as near to the central idea of the occasion in two hours as you did in two minutes."

Though it made no stir at the time it was delivered, Lincoln's Gettysburg Address has come to be considered one of the most eloquent and inspirational testaments in history to the ideals of freedom, equality, and democracy. It also transformed a scene that had been the sight of such horror and death into a lasting memorial to those who had sacrificed so much—and created a symbol of inspiration for the living to continue to fight for the noble cause of the preservation of the Union.

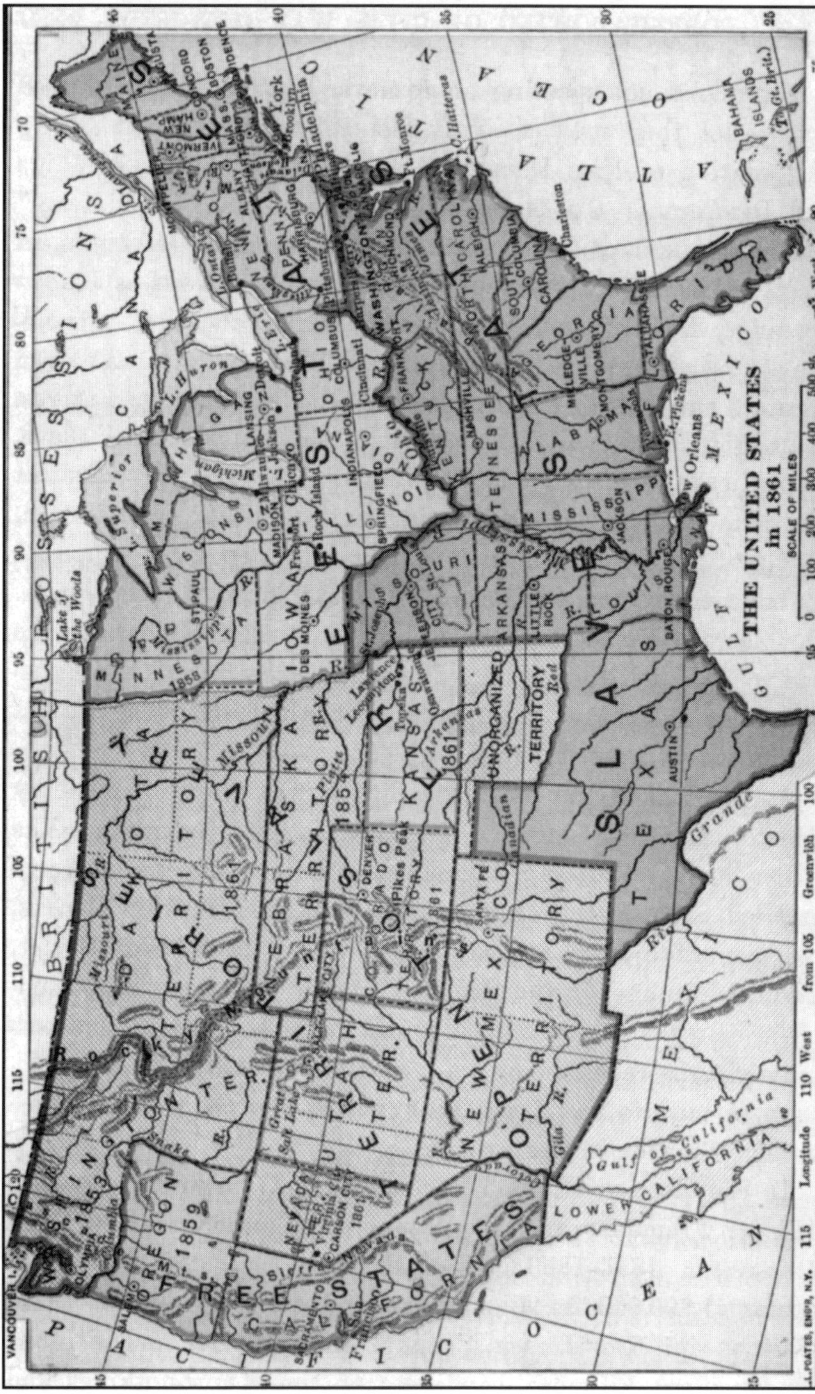

MAP OF THE UNITED STATES DURING THE CIVIL WAR

THE UNION TAKES THE OFFENSIVE

Gettysburg was the high point of the Confederate war effort and, also, the beginning of the end of the Confederate States of America.

The North was growing in military strength and economic power. Its losses had been huge, but it was not close to exhausting its manpower. Just as important, it had enough men and women, working in farms and factories, to keep crops growing and machines humming.

By contrast, the South was hard-pressed to absorb its manpower losses. As in the North, women had stepped forward to work in factories and maintain the farms, but there weren't enough of them. More significant was the loss of slave labor. Cotton, tobacco and rice were essential export crops for the Southern economy. These crops were labor intensive. Planters could not pay people to handpick cotton or harvest tobacco in the hot Southern sun. When the Union armies began operating in the South, the plantation system fell apart. By freeing slaves wherever they went, Union armies deprived the South of the labor it needed to sustain not only the war effort, but the export economy which the Confederacy needed to survive.

As long as Lee's leadership could keep the Army of Northern Virginia in the field, the Confederacy could be kept alive. After Gettysburg, however, it was

William Quantrill

evident that he could not defeat the Union forces; nor had he the manpower to keep the war going if the Union chose to fight.

With the Confederate armies in disarray, some Southerners began to advocate a strategy that would one day be called "guerrilla warfare." One such man was William Clarke Quantrill, who advocated giving no quarter to Union supporters and carrying the war to the Northern population behind military lines. Quantrill applied for a commission in the Confederate army, but his views were so extreme that his application was turned down. Nevertheless, Quantrill proclaimed himself a Confederate Colonel and organized a rebel force that included many men with criminal records. On August 21, 1863 Quantrill set out to avenge Gettysburg with an early morning raid on Lawrence, Kansas. Catching the small federal garrison still asleep, he and his men burned the city to the ground, killing 150 men, most of whom were civilians.

Quantrill's raid reflected a change in the nature of the Civil War. As the Union army began to move freely in the South, it began to target the Confederacy's economic infrastructure, destroying railroads and factories, seizing or burning crops and burning plantations that stood in its path. In response, Southerners began to desert the army in order to go home and protect their local communities.

While Lee and Meade engaged their armies at Gettsyburg, the Union and Confederate forces continued to do battle in the West. On June 26, 1863, Union Major General William S. Rosecrans began to move his army out of Murfreesboro, Tennessee towards Chattanooga. His opponent, General Braxton Bragg, having sent part of his army to defend Vicksburg, was outnumbered in force by three to two. When Rosecrans destroyed the railroad that Bragg needed to supply his troops in Chattanooga, Bragg had to abandon the city. Chattanooga was a railroad hub that was vital to the protection of Georgia and the Carolinas from a Union attack from the west. Lee sent a corps of troops led by General Longstreet to reinforce Bragg's army. On September 19 and 20, Bragg and Longstreet attacked Rosecrans's army along Chickamauga Creek, northeast of Chattanooga. Only a brave stand by bayonet-wielding Union troops under Major General George Thomas prevented Bragg from cutting Rosecrans's army in half and winning a decisive victory.

Bragg then laid siege to Chattanooga, stationing his troops on Lookout Mountain and Missionary Ridge above the Union encampment. A quick attack from the heights might have destroyed Rosecrans's army, but Bragg, like so many Civil War generals before him, bided his time. This enabled Lincoln to reorganize his western forces. Grant replaced Rosecrans as the General of the Army of Western Tennessee, while General William Sherman led troops from Vicksburg and Joseph Hooker led troops from the Army of the Potomac to reinforce Thomas's vulnerable position in Chattanooga.

On November 24, Thomas, fighting under Grant's command, attempted to break through the Confederate lines overlooking Chattanooga. The following

THE BATTLE OF CHICKAMAUGA

day, his troops broke through the Confederate's first line of defense below Missionary Ridge and, without any direct order, kept on going until they had driven the Confederates from the ridge line. The Rebels fled in disorganized fashion back into Georgia. Thomas's victory in Chattanooga was strategically more important than the victory at Gettysburg. Not only did Bragg forfeit the opportunity to destroy a Union army; his own defeat opened the way to the Union invasion of Georgia and the Carolinas. On November 30, Bragg resigned from his command of the Army of Tennessee and was replaced by General Joseph E. Johnston.

After Grant's success at Vicksburg, Lincoln came to believe he had found the one man capable of leading the Union forces to ultimate victory. Grant was summoned to the capital, and in March 1864, he was promoted to Lieutenant General and appointed commander-in-chief of the entire Union army. Confident in his western generals, Sherman and Thomas, Grant choose to station himself with the Army of the Potomac in order to lead another campaign against Lee's army. Grant's strategy was to keep fighting and flanking, relentlessly moving to the side of Lee's forces in the hope of finding a weakness, or wearing them down and making a final and successful end run towards Richmond. This was to be a war of attrition; understanding that the North had greater manpower and industrial resources, Grant planned to wear down Lee's army until it lacked the means to continue the fight.

Grant began his campaign to finish off the Army of Northern Virginia in early May of 1864 from his base camp near Culpepper, in the same part of eastern Virginia that Union armies had been contesting since the first Battle of Bull Run. With 100,000 men, Grant planned to march through the densely wooded area known as the Wilderness and force Lee into continuous battle in order to protect Richmond. At the same time, Grant sent Major General Benjamin Butler with about 30,000 men to march towards Richmond along the Southern bank of the James River. A third army, led by Major General Franz Sigel, was to march through the Shenandoah Valley, seize the important railroad hub of Lynchburg, and draw Lee's attention to the west and north. To battle these armies, Lee had 60,000 men under his own command, and 30,000 under the command of General Beauregard, stationed in Petersburg and Richmond.

On May 4 all the Union armies set out. Grant and the main force crossed the Rapidan River and were immediately attacked by Lee's forces. The Wilderness was an ideal place for Lee to fight because the dense forest made it impossible for Grant to consolidate his troops and take advantage of his overwhelming strength in manpower. Two days of skirmishing resulted in Grant losing about 18,000 men, including more than 2,000 dead.

Unlike previous Union commanders who, at this point, would have pulled back to lick their wounds, Grant pressed forward. He marched all night in order to capture the crossroads at the Spotsylvania Court House, which controlled a direct route to Richmond. The Battle of Spotsylvania lasted five days, from May 8-12. At one point, the Army of the Potomac broke through Lee's lines at the so-called "Bloody Angle," but after a solid day of hand-to-hand combat, the Union attack was broken. On May 11, Grant sent word to Washington: "I propose to fight it out along this line if it takes all summer."

Unfortunately, Grant would have to lead the fighting in the East almost alone. General Butler, advancing towards Richmond on the James, was

ULYSSES S. GRANT AND HIS GENERALS

UNION GENERAL SEDGWICK WAS KILLED AT THE BATTLE OF SPOTSYLVANIA

stopped by a small Confederate force at Bermuda Hundred. His army was no longer a threat to Richmond. General Sigel was also stopped by a smaller Confederate force at New Market in the Shenandoah. The only modest success was a cavalry raid that General Philip Sheridan led into the Richmond suburbs. It was beaten back, but Jeb Stuart, Lee's favorite cavalry officer, was killed in battle.

Despite heavy losses–2000 casualties a day–Grant kept moving his army westward in an effort to outflank Lee's army and find an opening towards Richmond. By maintaining an offensive, Grant successfully neutralized Lee's ability to maneuver his army and choose the site of battle.

On June 3, Grant tried a frontal assault against Lee's entrenched forces at Cold Harbor, along the Chickahominy River. The Union attackers were slaughtered; the Union forces lost nearly 7,000 men in less than an hour. Grant had now lost 60,000 men in the campaign, as many men as were in Lee's army. However, new troops filled the ranks. Lee's losses numbered about 25,000, but there were few new troops to meet his need for replacements.

After Cold Harbor, Grant crossed the James in mid-June and set his sights on Petersburg, a railroad junction important to keeping supplies flowing to Richmond. Despite an overwhelming advantage in troop strength and smart strategic planning, the Union's frontal assault on Petersburg was poorly coordinated and ineffective; General Beauregard managed to hold the defensive line until Lee's reinforcements arrived and the Union offensive ground to a standstill. On June 18, Grant called off the attack and began the siege of Petersburg.

The front was quiet until July, when a regiment of Pennsylvania coal miners from General Burnside's corps dug a 500-foot tunnel under the enemy's lines and planted four tons of black powder beneath a Confederate fort. On July 30, an explosion blew a huge gap in an otherwise impregnable defense system. However, Burnside's men bungled the assault through the breach; the Confederates quickly repaired the damage before heavy pressure could be applied, and the attack failed, with substantial losses. So the siege continued through the autumn and into the winter.

In a desperate effort to shift the tide, Lee had sent General Jubal Early on a raid through the Shenandoah Valley. On July 12, he approached the suburbs of Washington; but Grant had sent veteran units to protect the city and, with President Lincoln watching from a distance, the Confederates were beaten back. Just as important, Grant continued to put pressure on Petersburg; he was not distracted by Early's action.

On July 30, 1864, cavalrymen from Early's army raided Chambersburg, Pennsylvania and demanded a ransom of $500,000 in currency and $100,000 in gold. When the citizens refused, they burned down the town. A week later, General Philip Sheridan was placed in command of a new Army of the Shenandoah with orders to defeat Early and destroy the agricultural resources of the valley. Sheridan fulfilled his goal in September and October, defeating Early in battles at Winchester, Fisher's Hill, and most famously at Cedar Creek, Virginia, where Early's forces were in the process of routing Sheridan's troops as the general returned from a strategy session in Washington. With a furious 20-mile ride, Sheridan rallied his men, turned them around, and once and for all drove Early's army from the Valley. After his victories, Sheridan destroyed nearly all the farms, barns, mills, and livestock in the Valley.

During the fall of 1864 the presidential election was approaching, and for Lincoln and his government the news from Virginia was as gloomy as ever. The Union was suffering high casualties, and Lee was still in control of Richmond. Yet, his army was weakening, and Grant's long-term strategy was working. Moreover, in Georgia, Sherman's army was triumphant. As the new commander of an army of 100,000 troops, Sherman opened up a second front at the same time that Grant began his campaign in the Wilderness.

Like Grant, Sherman used a strategy of continuous fighting in an effort to outflank Joseph E. Johnston's army. Sherman's goal was to take control of

Union forces blow a huge gap in the Confederate defenses at Petersburg

the railroad line from Atlanta that Johnston was dependent upon for supplies. Though Johnston's army was able to win daily skirmishes, Sherman continuously maintained his flanking movements, forcing Johnston to move with him closer and closer to Atlanta.

Frustrated by Johnston's defensive maneuvers, Jefferson Davis replaced him with Major General John B. Hood, who promised to go on the offensive and stop Sherman's progress. Hood had experience commanding troops both in the West and under Lee in Virginia. However, his offensive against Sherman only caused casualties that the Confederacy could not afford, and Sherman continued to drive towards Atlanta, destroying all connecting railroads in the process. On September 2, Hood evacuated Atlanta and Sherman's troops took control of the city. Five days later, Sherman ordered all civilians to leave the city and then he burned it to the ground. "If the people raise a howl against my barbarity and cruelty, I will answer that war is war and not popularity seeking," Sherman said.

General William T. Sherman

Back in Washington, Lincoln was under fire from opposing factions in his own party. Hawkish radical Republicans criticized his leadership in the war and threatened to run the western explorer John C. Fremont as a third party candidate. In addition, Southern sympathizers who wanted to negotiate a peaceful settlement joined with Copperhead Democrats in nominating former General George McClellan for president. Though McClellan repudiated the Democratic peace plank, he continually attacked Lincoln's conduct of the war.

To win the broadest possible support for the war effort, the Republicans called their nominating convention the National Union Convention, and chose Senator Andrew Johnson of Tennessee for Vice President. A Democrat, Johnson had been the only member of Congress from a secessionist state to remain loyal to the Union. The Republican plank called for unconditional surrender from the Confederacy and a constitutional amendment to abolish slavery.

With most Northerners weary of the war and the battlefield news bleak, there was no certainty that Lincoln would be reelected. The president himself had doubts and was prepared to accept defeat. No country had ever allowed elections during a period of civil strife, but win or lose, Lincoln was determined to show that democracy could work even in such a time of trouble.

As it turned out, Sherman's capture of Atlanta and Sheridan's success in the Shenandoah Valley in the weeks leading up to the election buoyed Northern spirits and helped turn the tide in Lincoln's favor. His victory in the popular vote was small, 2,206,938 to McClellan's 1,803,787, but his electoral vote victory was decisive, 212 to 21.

The Confederacy, meanwhile, was faced with the problem of stopping Sherman in Georgia. In an attempt to retake the initiative, Hood moved his army back to Tennessee, intending to destroy Sherman's supply line and hoping to tempt the Union army into pursuit. Sherman refused to take the bait and, in October, took a bold step. He sent General George Thomas with troops from the Army of the Cumberland to contend with Hood; Sherman then took the greater portion of his army, some 60,000 men, and on November 15, 1864 began a march along a 60-mile swath, from Atlanta east to the sea.

Without any supplies of their own, Sherman's men lived off the land, seizing crops and cattle for their own consumption. They burned and destroyed everything else–plantation houses, barns, bridges, cotton gins, railroads, lumber mills, and factories. However, this was a disciplined and veteran army. Under Sherman's leadership, they focused on the destruction of property; very few acts of violence against civilians were reported. Sherman's army also liberated 40,000 slaves in Georgia, many of whom followed the army's path east. Sherman had not only abandoned his supply lines, but he also had no way to communicate his progress to Washington. "I know the hole he went in at," Lincoln explained to his advisors, "but I can't tell you what hole he will come out of."

Sherman's march, unchallenged by an organized Confederate army, led many Georgians to desert Hood and Lee and return home to fight Sherman. Lee remained pinned down in Petersburg and needed all his troops to defend Richmond. Hood's one option was to destroy Thomas's army in Tennessee and rush back to Georgia to fight Sherman. On November 30, Hood made contact with a part of Thomas's army at Franklin, Tennessee. Hood mounted a spectacular—and hopeless—assault on the Union line that cost more than 6,000 casualties. General John M. Schofield, the commander of the Union force, then joined up with Thomas at Nashville and in a two-day battle, on December 15–16, almost destroyed Hood's army, pushing the remnants back into Mississippi.

Without any Southern army to stop him, Sherman reached the coast below Savannah, Georgia on December 10; his forces then captured Fort McAllister and opened a supply route by sea. A 10,000–man Confederate garrison managed to destroy everything of value in Savannah–and slip away heading north–before Sherman's forces seized the city on December 22. Two days later, Sherman sent Lincoln a telegram offering Savannah to him as a Christmas gift. With Hood's army defeated and Lee pinned down in Virginia, it was now evident that the Confederacy's days were numbered.

THE END OF THE CONFEDERACY

On February 1, 1865 General Sherman's 60,000-man veteran army began its march north from Georgia into South Carolina. Two days later, Confederate representatives–including Vice President Stephens–again attempted to negotiate a settlement with President Lincoln. This time, Lincoln consented to meet with them, on a Union naval vessel off Hampton Roads, Virginia. However, the representatives' insistence that Confederate independence be the condition for peace was unacceptable. "The war will cease on the part of the Government, whenever it shall have ceased on the part of those who began it," Lincoln said. The Union represented the only legitimate government to Lincoln; the Confederates did not represent a country, but were

DEFENSIVE TRENCHES IN PETERSBURG

BATTLE WEARY UNION SOLDIERS AT PETERSBURG

merely Americans in temporary rebellion.

Meanwhile, Sherman was marching through South Carolina, taking revenge on the state that led the way to secession and started the war by firing on Fort Sumter. On February 17, Sherman's men burned the capital, Columbia, and the next day they forced the evacuation of Charleston. General Lee sent General Johnston, with as many troops as he could muster, into North Carolina to stop Sherman. Johnston met him at Bentonville on March 19-20, but the battle was indecisive and Johnston lacked the resources to continue fighting.

At the same time, in Virginia, Grant continued his siege of Petersburg. The necessity of protecting Richmond prevented General Lee from sending troops to stop Sherman. It also prevented Lee from doing what he did best, maneuvering his troops to confuse Union generals and strike at their weaknesses.

The siege of Petersburg saw the introduction of trench warfare. The Confederate troops were protected by rows of long trenches. Across an area of no-man's land, the Army of the Potomac had its own trenches. The only way to attack was by frontal assaults across the vacant area between the two armies. The army on the defense had an overwhelming advantage in this kind of conflict. Its firepower could mow down the attacking army running through the no-man's land; without cover, it was dangerous for the attackers even to stop to retrieve their dead or wounded.

Grant understood the futility of such attacks and, instead, kept extending his trenches in order to force Lee to stretch out his defenses. With 150,000 troops against Lee's 54,000, Grant could extend his lines for miles. Unable to fight a war of maneuvering, the shrinking size of Lee's army became a problem. In desperation, the Confederacy began talking about employing slaves in their army.

The issue was first raised more than a year earlier, in January 1864, by Major General Patrick Cleburne who, believing the Southern cause was otherwise doomed, wanted to free those slaves who would serve in the Confederate army. "Every patriot will freely give up…the Negro slave rather than be a slave himself," he argued. Jefferson Davis refused to consider this option when it was first presented but, later that year, on November 11, 1864, Davis himself proposed that the Confederate government

THE BATTLE OF FIVE FORKS

buy slaves from their owners and give the slaves their freedom in return for service in the Confederate army.

By this time, the Confederacy had less than 200,000 men under arms, one-third of the number in the Union army, and 100,000 less than the South had at the time of Vicksburg and Gettysburg. Desperate to alleviate the manpower shortage, Davis proposed purchasing 40,000 slaves to serve in noncombatant roles in the army, but the Confederate Congress refused to act.

Robert E. Lee also suggested that blacks would make better soldiers if they fought not as slaves, but as free men. However, to some Southerners, such talk threatened to undermine a major reason for the Confederate rebellion. "If slaves will make good soldiers," Howell Cobb, from Georgia, exclaimed, "our whole theory of slavery is wrong." On February 10, 1865, the Confederacy passed a law recruiting slaves as soldiers. However, the desperate action came too late.

With victory now certain, President Lincoln began to think about government policy after the conclusion of the war. He was under pressure from radical Republicans who wanted the South, especially the slaveholders, to pay a high price for its rebellion. Lincoln's instinct, however, was to bring the nation together. "Let up easy," he advised Sherman and Grant at a meeting with his two generals as the war was ending. Lincoln wanted to disband the Confederate armies and allow the soldiers to go back home without being humiliated or punished. In his second inaugural address, March 4, 1865, the president expressed his ideal of victory with compassion:

"... With malice toward none; with charity for all; with firmness in the right, as God gives us to see the right, let us strive on to finish the work we are in; to bind up the nation's wounds; to care for him who shall have borne the battle, and for his widow, and his orphan -- to do all which may achieve and cherish a just and lasting peace among ourselves and with all nations."

On March 25, General Lee tried to break the siege of Petersburg with a surprise early morning attack on a Union position, Fort Stedman, east of the town. His troops captured the position, but lacked the manpower to hold it. A Union counterattack sent the Confederates back to their trenches. At the end of March, General Sheridan, having cleaned the Confederate army out of the Shenandoah Valley, brought his troops to Petersburg. On April 1, he moved 12,000 mounted troops towards Five Forks, a road and railroad junction that Lee needed to keep open in order to supply his troops in Petersburg and defend Richmond. A Confederate detachment, led by General George Pickett, tried to contain Sheridan. Badly outnumbered, they were mauled by Sheridan's soldiers and 5,000 Confederates were taken prisoner.

By now, the Confederate lines were so stretched that Grant believed he could attack their center. On April 2, a frontal assault broke through the Confederate lines and entered Petersburg. That night Lee ordered the evacuation of Petersburg and Richmond, which was now defenseless. The Confederates burned their own factories and mills before leaving. On April 3, Union forces entered the city and brought the fires under control. Lincoln came the next day and spent a moment sitting at Jefferson Davis's desk.

Lee's plan was to move his tired army South and join General Johnston in fighting Sherman. In evacuating Richmond, Confederate war-planners were unable to organize shipments of food and supplies for Lee's battered army. Moreover, Grant, true to his strategy, would not allow Lee to break away. When, on April 9, Sheridan's troops blocked the only route Lee could take in order to link up with General Johnston, Lee knew the war was over.

Lee had the choice—Confederate leaders had even discussed it —of moving his army west into the Appalachian hills and engaging in guerrilla warfare.

THE CITY OF RICHMOND BURNS ON APRIL 3,1865

John Wilkes Booth Assassinates President Lincoln

However, he refused to take that option. "It is our duty to live," he said, "for what will become of the women and children of the South, if we are not here to support and protect them." Instead, with Union forces preparing to make a final attack, he accepted General Grant's request for Lee to surrender.

On April 9, 1865, the two generals met to discuss terms at Appomattox Court House, about 20 miles east of Lynchburg. Lee arrived in his full-dress uniform. Grant was dressed in a private's shirt and, unlike Lee, he did not carry a sword. Grant wrote the terms of surrender on a piece of paper. Officers and men would be paroled; officers were allowed to keep their side arms, and soldiers were permitted to take a horse or mule back home with them to work their farms. When the Confederate soldiers began to turn in their weapons, the Union army broke into cheers. Grant ordered the cheering to stop. "The war is over," he said. "The rebels are our countrymen again."

On the night of April 11, President Lincoln spoke from a White House window to a large crowd delirious with news of the Union victory. While the crowd expected–and wanted–a speech celebrating the end of the rebellion, Lincoln instead gave them a sober, unemotional speech about the difficult job that lay ahead in building a new union and a new freedom.

Three days later, on Good Friday, Lincoln met with his cabinet. He ordered an end to the naval blockade, and discussed details with his advisors about a policy for peaceful reconstruction. That night the president, his wife, and two guests attended the production of the play *Our American Cousin* at the Ford Theater in Washington. Shortly after 10:00 p.m., an actor named John Wilkes Booth, a bitter pro-slavery, Confederate supporter, entered the presidential box and shot Lincoln once in the back of the head. Mortally wounded, the president was carried across the street to a lodging house where he died the next morning. Booth, who had jumped to the stage after firing the shot, injuring his leg in the process, escaped.

The country was stunned and horrified. The war department offered a $50,000 reward for Booth's capture. In the investigation of the killing, it was revealed that Booth was the leader of a plot to assassinate government leaders as revenge against the North for the South's defeat. (The night of Lincoln's murder, one of the conspirators had tried and failed to kill Secretary of State William H. Seward at his home.)

On April 26, Booth was cornered in a Virginia barn by Union soldiers and was killed. Seven of Booth's accomplices–six men and a woman–were rounded up and quickly tried and convicted by a military court. Three were sentenced to life imprisonment, and four were sentenced to death, including Mrs. Mary Surratt, who owned a boardinghouse where the conspirators had lodged and made their plans. The four were hanged on July 7, 1865.

While much of the country was preoccupied with the capture of the assassins, the South technically still had an army at war. Although Lee had surrendered his Army of Northern Virginia, General Joseph Johnston was still in the field trying to contain Sherman, while Jefferson Davis and what was left of his government, fled across the Carolinas into Georgia, still urging rebel resistance. However, when Johnston learned of Lee's surrender, he realized the futility of continuing the fight; he and Sherman met near Durham Station, North Carolina on April 17 to work out a surrender. The final Southern detachment, a western army commanded by General Edmund Kirby Smith, surrendered on May 26 to Union forces in New Orleans.

Jefferson Davis, meanwhile, tried to escape to his home in Mississippi. On May 10, he was captured by federal cavalry while hiding out near Irwinville, Georgia. Davis was imprisoned for two years in Fort Monroe, Virginia. Despite demands by many Northerners that he be tried for treason, he was released in the general amnesty of 1868 and, in poor health, spent the rest of his life at his home in Mississippi.

John Wilkes Booth

AFTERMATH

In terms of the number of casualties in relation to men in service, the Civil War was the bloodiest war in American history. More than 140,000 Union soldiers died in battle, and another 220,000 died of diseases and other causes; the South lost more than 160,000 in battle and to other causes. In addition, hundreds of thousands of men on both sides were wounded, and many of them were left permanently disabled. The loss of men in the prime of their life was felt in cities, small towns, and on farms throughout the country.

Following President Lincoln's assassination, Vice President Andrew Johnson, a Democrat from Tennessee, became president. With few political skills and no political standing–he was considered a traitor by many in the South, and reviled by many radical Republicans–Johnson had to heal the wounds of war with a divided Congress in which he had few allies.

The North was booming, but the South was devastated. In addition to losing one-quarter of its white men of military age, the war also destroyed two-fifths of Southern livestock, a similar proportion of its factories and railroads, and two-thirds of the region's wealth.

Plantation crops–cotton, tobacco and rice–were the basis for the South's economy. However, with much of the land destroyed, and without slaves, the plantation economy could not function. On the other hand, while the slaves were free, they had no home, no land, and no money or other assets to start a new life. Because of the slave system, most were uneducated and unskilled in anything but manual labor. The harshness of the economic situation, the cause of much bitterness among both Southern whites and blacks, helped contribute greatly to the difficult period of Reconstruction that was to follow.

The national debate over Reconstruction had actually begun during the latter stages of the war. Even had Lincoln lived, there would have been a major dispute over the process of reunifying the country. On what terms should the defeated Confederacy be reunited with the Union? Who should establish these terms, the Congress or the Executive branch? What should the place of blacks be in the political and social life of a readmitted South? Without Lincoln,

ANDREW JOHNSON

under a new president distrusted by both Southerners and Northerners, these issues became even more difficult to manage.

In the aftermath of the war, both North and South would undergo a great upheaval that would last for decades. Indeed, the effects of the Civil War would influence the political, social, and economic life of the United States well into the 20th century—and the legacy of slavery would continue to be felt throughout American society more than 135 years after the end of the war.

WHERE TO GO

This section is designed as your guide to parks, historic sites, museums, and interpretive centers in the United States and its territories, where you can go to see what life was like in the historical period covered by *The Civil War.*

At these sites, you can see where many of the events in the book actually took place, or view exhibits relating to the everyday lives of the people who lived and worked in America in the period from 1861 to 1865 and beyond.

1. Fort Morgan Historic Site
51 Highway 180 West
Gulf Shores, AL 36542
(334) 540-7202

Fort Morgan, controlling access to the port at Mobile, allowed Confederate trading ships to run the Union blockade. On August 23, 1864, a Union fleet led by Admiral David Farragut ran the torpedo mines protecting the harbor, and captured the fort.

2. First White House of the Confederacy
644 Washington Avenue
Montgomery, AL 36130
(334) 242-1861

This historic house was the home of Jefferson Davis and his family in 1861 when Montgomery was the first capital of the Confederacy. The museum features furniture and personal property of President Davis, artifacts from the war, and furnishings of the period.

3. Pea Ridge National Military Park
15930 Hwy. 62
Garfield, AR 72751
(501) 451-8122
www.nps.gov/peri

Site of the Union victory in a March 1862 battle t that kept Missouri in the Union. The restored Elkhorn Tavern was the site of the heaviest fighting. A part of the Cherokee " Trail of Tears" runs through the park.

4. Arkansas Post National Memorial
1741 Old Post Road
Gillett, AR 72055
870-548-2207
www.gov.nps./ arpo

Museum exhibits depict history of Arkansas from the present back to archeological times. Includes Fort Hindman, an earthen fortification built by the Confederates and destroyed by Union forces in January, 1863.

5. Old State House Museum
300 W. Markham St.
Little Rock, AR 72201
(501) 324–9685
www.oldstatehouse.com

A collection of Civil War artifacts, including Confederate battle flags.

6. Prairie Grove Battlefield State Park
14262 W. Hwy. 62
Prairie Grove, AR 72753
(501) 846–2990

This Civil War Park Museum is located on the site of the December 1862 Battle of Prairie Grove. A collection of artifacts, exhibits, and documents from the war.

7. Ford's Theatre National Historic Site
511 10th St. N.W.
Washington, DC 20024
(202) 426-6924
www.nps.gov/foth/

The theater in which Abraham Lincoln was shot contains a museum about the assassination. Across the street, the Petersen House, where Lincoln was carried, has been restored to depict the site of the president's death.

8. Frederick Douglass National Historic Site
1411 W Street, S.E.
Washington, DC 20020
(202) 426-5961
www.cr.nps.gov/csd/exhibits/douglass

The home of Frederick Douglas from 1877 to 1895, exhibitions commemorate the life of the foremost African–American leader in the fight against slavery and the struggle for human rights.

9. Lincoln Memorial
23rd Street, Potomac Park, N.W.
Washington, D.C.

The national memorial to President Lincoln, dedicated in 1922, is located near the Potomac River on The Mall. Built of white marble in the classical Greek style, it contains a statue of a seated Lincoln, sculptured by Daniel Chester French, looking out towards the Capitol.

10. Judah P. Benjamin Confederate Memorial
Plantation State Historic Site
3708 Patten Avenue
Ellenton, FL 34222
(941) 723-4536
www.dep.state.fl.us/parks

The plantation home of sugar planter Robert Gamble is also the location of a memorial to Judah Philip Benjamin, known as "the brains of the Confederacy. A senator from Louisiana, Benjamin served the Confederacy first as Attorney-General, then as Secretary of War, and finally as Secretary of State.

11. Museum of Southern History
4304 Herschel Street
Jacksonville, FL 32210
(904) 388-3574

Museum of the culture and lifestyle of the antebellum South and the Confederate period. Exhibits include black soldiers in the Confederate service.

12. Civil War Soldiers Museum
108 S. Palafox Place
Pensacola, FL 32501
(850) 469-1900
www.cwmuseum.org

Museum dedicated to the Civil War soldier includes exhibits on everyday life as well as medical care and treatment of the wounded.

13. Andersonville National Historic Site
496 Cemetery Road
Andersonville, GA 31711
(229) 924-0343
www.nps.gov/ande

The site of the Andersonville Prison, it includes the National Prisoner of War Museum, with exhibits on themes common to all prisoners of war.

14. Atlanta Cyclorama
800-C Cherokee Avenue, S.E.
Atlanta, GA 30315
(404) 658–7625
www.BCAAtlanta.org

Civil War museum devoted to the battle of Atlanta. Contains a 42- ft. high, 365-ft. in circumference cyclorama depicting the decisive battle between Sherman's Union army and Hood's Confederate forces.

15. Atlanta Historical Society
Atlanta History Center
130 W. Paces Ferry Road, N.W.
Atlanta, GA 30305
(404) 814–4000
www.atlhist.org

Atlanta History Museum includes Civil War and African-American history as well as the memorabilia of Margaret Mitchell, author of *Gone With the Wind.* The site contains restored houses and period gardens.

16. Port Columbus Civil War Naval Center
South Commons at Victory Drive
Columbus, GA 31902
(706) 324–7334
www.portcolumbus.org

Museum of Civil War naval operations on display.

17. Confederate Museum
456 Alexander Street
Crawfordsville, GA 30631
(706) 456–2221
www.g.-net/ ~ ahssp

Museum in restored home of Confederate Vice President Alexander Stephens has exhibits on Stephens and the Civil War period.

18. Chickamauga–Chattanooga National Military Park
U.S. 27, S.
Fort Oglethorpe, GA 30742
(706) 866-9241
www.nps.gov/chch

Commemorates Union General William Thomas's decisive victories at Chickamauga Creek and Lookout Mountain in Chattanooga, Tennessee.

19. Kennesaw Civil War Museum
2829 Cherokee Street
Kennesaw, GA 30144
(770) 427-2117
www.ngeorgia.com/history/kcwm.shtml

Civil War museum emphasizing railroads of the period.

20. Kennesaw Mountain National Battlefield Park
900 Kennesaw Mountain Dr.
Kennesaw, GA 30152
(770) 427–4686
www.nps.gov.kemo

Battle site of Confederate General Joseph Johnston's failed attempt to stop Union General William Tecumseh Sherman's invasion of Georgia in 1864.

21. Fort McAllister
3894 Fort McAllister Road
Richmond Hill, GA 31324
(912) 727-2339

Restored earthworks of Confederate Civil War fort near Savannah captured by William Tecumseh Sherman's Union forces during their march to the sea.

22. Fort Pulaski National Monument
U.S. Hwy. 80 E.
Savannah, GA 31410
U.S. 80 East towards Tybee Island
(912) 786-5787
www.nps.gov/fopu/

Restored Confederate fort captured in April, 1862 by Union troops using experimental rifled cannons that made brick fortifications obsolete.

23. Old Fort Jackson
1 Ft. Jackson Rd.
Savannah, GA 31404
(912) 232–3945
www. chsgeorgia.org

Artifacts relating to Fort Jackson and the history of Savannah.

24. Georgia's Stone Mountain Park
Hwy. 78
Stone Mountain, GA 30086
(404) 498–5690 & 5600
www.stonemountainpark.org

A collection of Civil War artifacts set among gardens and nature trails.

25. Robert Toombs House
216 E. Robert Toombs Avenue
Washington, GA 30673
(706) 678–7515

Home of the Confederacy's first Secretary of State, who later served as commander of a Georgia brigade on the Virginia front.

26. U.S. Grant's Home State Historic Site
500 Bouthillier Street
Galena, IL 61036
(815) 777-3310
www.state.il.us/hpa

Exhibitions of Grant's life in Galena with restored buildings from pre-Civil War period.

27. Lincoln Home National Historic Site
426 S. Seventh Street
Springfield, IL 62701
(217) 492-4241
www.nps.gov/liho

Restored home of Abraham and Mary Lincoln from 1844 until Lincoln's election as president commemorates his life as a family man, lawyer, and presidential candidate.

28. Lincoln Tomb Historic Site
Oak Ridge Cemetery
Springfield, IL 62702
(217) 782-2717

The burial place of the nation's sixteenth president, his wife, Mary, and their sons, Edward, William, and Thomas.

29. The Lincoln Museum
200 E. Berry St.
Fort Wayne, IN 46801
(219) 455–3864

Exhibits and a collection of artifacts relating to the Civil War and the presidency of Abraham Lincoln.

30 Indiana War Memorials
431 N. Meridian St.
Indianapolis, IN 46204
(317) 232-7615

Exhibits and a collection of artifacts from the Civil War.

31. Lincoln Boyhood National Memorial
Highway 162
Lincoln City, IN 47552
(812) 937-4541
www.nps.gov/libo

The family farm where Abraham Lincoln grew up is a museum of the president's formative years.

32. Riverview at Hobson Grove
1100 W. Main Avenue
Bowling Green, KY 42102
(502) 843–5565
www.bgky.org/riverview.htm

A collection of artifacts in an historic house and museum used to store Confederate munitions during the Civil War.

33. Columbus-Belmont Civil War Museum
Columbus-Belmont State Park
350 Park Road
Columbus, KY 42032
(270) 677–2327
www.kystateparks.com

Civil War artifacts and dioramas.

34. Behringer-Crawford Museum
1600 Montague Road, Devou Park
Covington, KY 41012
(606) 491-4003

Museum exhibits on the Civil War in northern Kentucky and the Ohio River Valley.

35. Abraham Lincoln Birthplace National Historic Site
2995 Lincoln Farm Road
Hodgenville, KY 42748
(270) 358–3137
www.nps.gov/albi

The log cabin in which Abraham Lincoln was born is enshrined in a marble and granite memorial.

36. Jefferson Davis Monument State Park
Highway 68
Hopkinsville, KY 42240
(270) 886-1765

Commemorates birthplace and career of the Confederate president.

37. Perryville Battle Museum
1825 Battlefield Road
Perryville, KY 40468
(606) 332–8631
www.state.ky.usa/agencies/parks/perryvil

Museum and self-guided walking tour of the 1862 battle of Perryville, where Union forces under General Buell stopped General Bragg's planned invasion of Ohio.

38. Confederate Museum
929 Camp Street
New Orleans, LA 70130
(504) 523–4522
ww.confederatemuseum.com

The Civil War in Louisiana with displays of the personal effects of Jefferson Davis, Generals Beauregard, Bragg, Lee, and other Confederate leaders.

39. Baltimore Civil War Museum
President Street Station
601 President Street
Baltimore, MD 21202
(410) 385-5188

History of the underground railroad and the Civil War in Baltimore in an historic railroad station built around 1850.

40. Fort McHenry National Monument and Historic Shrine
End of E. Fort Avenue
Baltimore, MD 21230
(410)962–4290
www. nps.gov/fomc

This historic 1812 fort, site of the bombardment that inspired Francis Scott Key to write "The Star Spangled Banner," also served during the Civil War as a Union prison camp for Confederate soldiers and sympathizers.

41. Maryland Historical Society
201 W. Monument Street
Baltimore, MD 21201
(410) 685–3750
www.mdhs.org

Among this museum's exhibits and collection of artifacts is a Civil War gallery.

42. Surratt House Museum
9118 Brandywine Road
Clinton, MD 20735
(301) 868–1121
www.surratt.org

The boarding house run by Mrs. Mary Surratt, where John Wilkes Booth and his conspirators lodged as they plotted the assassination of President Lincoln and other northern government leaders, contains a collection of archival and photographic material relating to the assassination and the Civil War.

43. Monocacy National Battlefield
4801 Urbana Pike
Frederick, MD 21704
(301) 662-3515
www.nps.gov/mono/mo_visit.htm

Battle site of the last Confederate attempt to attack Washington, D.C. On July 9, 1864 Confederate General Jubal Early was stopped by Union forces commanded by General Lew Wallace.

44. National Museum of Civil War Medicine
48 E. Patrick Street
Frederick, MD 21701
(301) 695-1864
www.CivilWar.Med.org

Museum devoted to the study and exhibits of medicine and health care during the Civil War.

45. Clara Barton National Historic Site
5801 Oxford Road
Glen Echo, MD 20812
(301) 492–6245
www.nps.gov.clba

Home and office of Clara Barton, the founder of the American Red Cross, and, during the Civil War, known as the "Angel of the Battlefield" for her care of the wounded. Now a museum commemorating her life and work.

46. Antietam National Battlefield Site
Route 65 N.
Sharpsburg, MD 21782
(301) 432-5124
www.nps.gov/anti

Museum and self-guided walking tour mark the 1862 Battle of Antietam, a Union victory that stopped Lee's first attempted invasion of the North and enabled Lincoln to issue the Emancipation Proclamation. The Antietam National Cemetery is part of the battlefield site.

47. Springfield Armory National Historic Site
One Armory Square
Springfield, MA 01105
(413) 734-8551
www.nps.gov/index.html

Housed in an 1850 arsenal, an important Union facility during the Civil War, this museum has an extensive weapons collection, including one of the largest small arms collections in the world.

48. Beavoir, Jefferson Davis Home and Presidential Library
2244 Beach Street
Biloxi, MS 39531
(228) 338–9074
www.beavoir.org

The home of Jefferson Davis contains his library and papers, as well as memorabilia from his life as plantation owner, senator, and Confederate president. The site also has a Civil War museum and a historic cemetery.

49. Florewood River Plantation
Fort Loring Road
Greenwood, MS 38930
(662)455–3821

Artifacts and exhibits located in a history museum on an 1860 plantation.

50. Grand Gulf Military State Park Museum
Rt 3 (Grand Gulf Road)
Port Gibson, MS 39150
(601) 437–5911
www.grandgulfpark.state.ms.us

Military museum and historic site contains Civil War relics and reenactments of battles.

51. Brices Cross Roads National Battlefield
2680 Natchez Trace Parkway
Tupelo, MS 38804
(800) 305-7417 or (662) 680-4025
www.nps.gov/tupe

Site of July 1864 battle in which Confederate General Nathan Bedford Forrest captured Union supplies but failed to destroy the railroad supplying Union General Sherman on his march into Georgia.

52. Cedar Grove Mansion Inn
2200 Oak Street
Vicksburg, MS 39180
(601) 636–1000
www.cedargroveinn.com

A southern mansion located at the site of the siege of Vicksburg; among its interesting artifacts is a Civil War cannonball embedded in a parlor wall.

53. Old Court House Museum
1008 Cherry Street, Court Square
Vicksburg, MS 39183
(601) 636–0741

Museum housed in the 1858 Old Warren County Courthouse contains Civil War and antebellum South artifacts.

54. Vicksburg National Military Park–Cairo Museum
3201 Clay Street
Vicksburg, MS 39180
(601) 636-0583
www.nps.gov/vick

A 16– mile tour through Union and Confederate battle lines from the 6-week siege of Vicksburg. The site includes the restored USS *Cairo,* a Union ironclad gunboat raised from the

Mississippi River in 1964, a museum, and the Vicksburg National Cemetery.

55. Rosemont Plantation
Hwy. 24 East
Woodville, MS 39669
(601) 888-6809

Family home of Jefferson Davis houses collection of family artifacts and has reconstructed plantation buildings.

56. Confederate Memorial State Historic Site
211 W. First Street
Higginsville, MO 64037
(660) 584-2853

The site of a home for Confederate soldiers, commemorates the Confederate cause in Missouri.

57. John Wornall House
146 W. 61 Terrace
Kansas City, MO 64113
(816) 444–1858

Historic Greek Revival c.1858 home used as a hospital during the Civil War.

58. Battle of Lexington State Historic Site
Ext. Hwy. 13
Lexington, MO 64067
(816) 259–4654
www.digitalhistory.com/school/battleoflexing tonathistoricsite

Historic house and battlefield located at the site of the Battle of Hemp Bales.

59. Civil War Museum of LoneJack, Jackson County
301 S. Bynum Road
Lone Jack, MO 64070
(816) 566-2272

Museum has exhibits on the struggle by Union and Confederate forces for the control of Missouri, emphasizing the history of Jackson County.

60. Fort Davidson State Historic Site
Hwy. 21 and Hwy. V
Pilot Knob, MO 63663
(314) 546–3454

Historic site at the 1864 Battle of Pilot Knob.

61. General Sweeney's Museum
5228 S. State Highway ZZ
Republic, MO 65738
(417) 732-1224
www.civilwarmuseum.com

Museum of the Civil War in the Trans-Mississippi West includes exhibits of "Bloody Kansas" and the political and military struggle to keep Missouri in the Union.

62. Wilson's Creek National Battlefield
Hwy. ZZ and Farm Road
Republic, MO 65738
(417) 732-2662
www.nps.gov/wicr

Self-guided tour of 1861 battle site, the first Civil War battle west of the Mississippi River, a Confederate victory in Missouri that set the stage for a more decisive Union victory at Pea Ridge.

63. Ulysses S. Grant National Historic Site
7400 Grant Road
St. Louis, MO 63123
(314) 842-3298
www.nps.gov/ulsg

"White Haven," the home of Ulysses S. Grant and his wife Julia Dent Grant, contains exhibits of Grant as family man, general, and president.

64. John Brown Farm State Historic Site
John Brown Road
Lake Placid, NY 12946
(518) 523–3900
www.nysparks.com

The 1855 house occupied by John Brown and his family while he carried on his antislavery campaigns. Brown is also buried at the site.

65. General Grant National Memorial
Riverside Drive and W. 122nd St.
New York, NY 10027
(212) 666-1640
www.nps.gov/gegr

The largest mausoleum in North America, it contains the tomb of Ulysses S. Grant and his wife, as well as historical exhibitions about his life as a Civil War general and as the nation's eighteenth president.

66. Bentonville Battle State Historic Park
5466 Harper House Road
Four Oaks, NC 27524
(910) 594-0789
www. ah.dcr.state.nc.us/sections/hs/bentonvi/bentonvi.htm

Site of 1865 last-ditch attempt of Confederate army to stop General Sherman's march through the Carolinas. Site contains a Union field hospital and Union trenches.

67. Fort Fisher State Historic Site
U.S. Hwy. 421–1610
Fort Fisher Boulevard
Kure Beach, NC 28449
(910) 458–5538

A collection of artifacts and memorabilia on this site of the ruins and remains of the Civil War fort.

68. Grant's Birthplace State Memorial
U.S. 52 and State Rte. 232
Point Pleasant, OH 45153
(513) 553-4911

Restored cottage where General Grant was born with exhibits commemorating his life as military leader and president.

69. Pennsylvania Military Museum
Rtes. 322 and 45
Boalsburg, PA 16827
(814) 466–6263
www. psu.edu/dept/aerospace/museum/

This museum contains a collection of Pennsylvania military history, including Civil War regiment histories with unit rosters.

70. Gettysburg National Military Park
97 Taneytown Road
Gettysburg, PA 17325
(717) 334-1124
www.nps.gov/gett

The site of the most important battle of the Civil War and the National Cemetery where President Lincoln delivered his Gettysburg Address. The Park encompasses 6,000 acres and has 26 miles of park roads, and contains more than 1,400 monuments, markers, and memorials.

71. Gettysburg Soldiers National Museum
777 Baltimore Street
Gettysburg, PA 17325
(717) 334-4890

Military museum commemorating the soldiers who fought at Gettysburg.

72. James Buchanan Foundation for the Preservation of Wheatland
1120 Marietta Avenue
Lancaster, PA 17603
(717) 392–8721
www.wheatland.org

The home of James Buchanan, the nation's fifteenth president, is a seventeen-room federal-style brick mansion that has been fully restored.

73. The Civil War Library and Museum
1805 Pine Street
Philadelphia, PA 19103
(215) 735–8196
www.libertynet.org/cwlm

Restored 1857 house with display of weapons, uniforms, and personal memorabilia of Civil War soldiers.

74. Avery Research Center of African-American History and Culture
125 Bull Street
College of Charleston
Charleston, SC 29424
(843) 953-7609
www.cofc.edu/~acerey.rsc

Museum of African-American history in the Carolina low county region.

75. South Carolina Confederate Relic Room and Museum
World War Memorial Building
920 Sumter Street
Columbia, SC 29201
(803) 898–8095
www.state.su.us/crr

This museum contains relics from all periods of South Carolina history.

76. Hampton County Historical Museum
702 1st West, 601 South
Hampton, SC 29924
(803) 943-5484

Military museum with exhibitions from all eras, including a strong Civil War collection.

77. Fort Sumter National Monument
1214 Middle Street
Sullivan's Island, SC 29482
(843) 883-3123
www.nps.gov/fosu

Reachable by boat from Charleston Harbor, this site includes both Fort Moultrie as well as Fort Sumter. Self-guided tours and exhibits recreate the first battle of the Civil War.

78. Tennessee Civil War Museum
3914 St. Elmo Avenue
Chattanooga, TN 37409
(423) 821–4954
www.tncivilwarmuseum.com

This collection features a history of the Civil War, both North and South.

79. Fort Donelson National Battlefield
120 Fort Donelson Road
Dover, TN 37058
(931) 232-5706
www.nps.gov/fodo

The site of an important Union victory in February 1862 contains a military cemetery, the fort, and the hotel in which the Confederates surrendered to General Grant.

80. Andrew Johnson National Historic Site
101 North College Street
Greeneville, TN 37743
(423) 638–3551
www.nps.gov/anjo

The homestead of Lincoln's vice president and the nation's seventeenth president. An educational display of the events leading up to his impeachment provides an opportunity for visitors to cast their own vote for or against impeachment.

81. Abraham Lincoln Library and Museum, Lincoln Memorial University
Hwy. 25E. Cumberland Gap Pkwy.
Harrowgate, TN 37752
(423) 869–6235
www.lmunet.edu/museum/index.html

A collection of 20,000 artifacts, including materials on President Lincoln and the Civil War.

82. Confederate Memorial Hall—Bleak House
3148 Kingston Pike SW
Knoxville, TN 37919
(865) 522-2371

Civil War memorabilia and records of Confederate soldiers.

83. Stones River National Battlefield
3501 Old Nashville Highway
Murfreesboro, TN 37129
(615) 893-9501
www.nps.gov/stri

Site of the Battle of Stones River (or Murfreesboro) in December 1862 and January 1863 where Union General Rosecrans forced the withdrawal of Confederate General Bragg and opened middle Tennessee to Union control. Site includes Stones River National Cemetery, the Hazen Brigade Monument, and portions of Fortress Rosecrans, an earthen fort.

84. Belle Meade Plantation
5025 Harding Road
Nashville, TN 37205
(615) 356–0501
www.citysearch/nas/plantation

Site of the Belle Meade Mansion, situated on a 24-acre, 19th -century thoroughbred farm. Includes 7 historic outbuildings, and Civil War and antebellum memorabilia.

85. Shiloh National Military Park
1055 Pittsburg Landing Rd
Shiloh,TN 38376
(901) 689 5275

Site of the April 1862 Battle of Shiloh, the bloodiest battle on the North American continent up until that time, includes a museum, battlefield markers, the Shiloh National Cemetery, and Indian artifacts.

86. Fort Bliss Museum
Pleasonton and Sheridan Roads
Fort Bliss, TX 79916
(915) 568–6940

This history museum is located on the site of a fort held alternately by Union and Confederate forces during the Civil War. Its collection contains military hardware and uniforms as well as early Southwest domestic items and Indian craft.

87. Museum of Southern History
14070 Southwest Freeway
Sugarland, TX, 77478
(281) 269-7171

Museum includes exhibits on life in the Confederacy and on Civil War battles.

88. Fort Ward Museum and Historic Site
4301 W. Braddock Road
Alexandria, VA 22304
(703)838-4848
www.ci.alexandria.va.us/oha/fortward

Museum of a Civil War fort built in 1861 to protect Washington D.C. from Confederate attack.

89. Appomattox Court House National Historical Park
Hwy. 24
Appomattox, VA 24522
(804) 352-8987
www.nps.gov/apco

A historic village museum on the site where General Robert E. Lee surrendered his Army of Northern Virginia to General Ulysses S. Grant's Army of the Potomac, ending the Civil War.

90. Arlington House, The Robert E. Lee Memorial
Arlington National Cemetery
Arlington, VA 22211
(703) 557–0613
www.arho.nps.gov

Located inside the cemetery, the 30-year residence of General Robert E. Lee, a house built by George Washington Parke Custis, foster son of George Washington, has been restored to its 1861 appearance as a national memorial to General Lee.

91. Museum of Culpeper History
803 South Main Street
Culpeper, VA 22701
(540) 829-1749
www.culpepermuseum.com

Culpeper County was the site of the battles of Cedar Mountain and Brandy Station. The Army of the Potomac camped there in 1863-1864. The museum offers photo exhibits and memorabilia, as well as tours of battle sites.

92. Casemate Museum
20 Bernard Road
Fort Monroe, VA 23651
(757) 727–3391

This military museum is located on the site where Confederate President Jefferson Davis was imprisoned after the Civil War. Exhibits also include documents on the ironclad vessels *Monitor* and *Merrimack*, as well as artifacts on notable Civil War figures.

93. Fredericksburg & Spotsylvania National Military Park
120 Chatham Lane
Fredericksburg, VA 22405
(540) 371-0802
www.nps.gov/ffrsp

The park links the Chancellorsville, Fredericksburg, Spotsylvania Court House and Wilderness battle sites. The Jackson Shrine commemorates the life of Confederate General Thomas "Stonewall" Jackson.

94. Lee Chapel and Museum
Washington and Lee University
Lexington, VA 24450
(540) 463-8768

Robert E. Lee became president of Washington University after the Civil War. The school was later renamed Washington and Lee. Museum contains artifacts from Lee's life as Civil War general and university president.

95. Stonewall Jackson House
8 E. Washington Street
Lexington, VA 24450
(540) 463–2552
www.stonewalljackson.org

Family home of the noted Confederate general has a museum with exhibitions of his life and times.

96. Manassas National Battlefield Park
6511 Sudley Road (Rt. 234)
Manassas, VA 20109
(703) 361–1339
www.nps.gov/mana

The 5000-acre site of the 1861 and 1862 battles of Manassas (or Bull Run) includes museum, battlefield tours, and markers.

97. Belle Grove Plantation
336 Belle Grove Road
Middletown, VA 22645
(540) 869–2028

The 1864 Civil War Battle of Cedar Creek was fought on the grounds of this historic house, which served as the headquarters of Union Army General Philip Sheridan.

98. New Market Battlefield State Historic Park
New Market, VA 22844
(540) 740–3101
www.vmi.edu/museum/nm

Site of 1864 Battle of New Market commemorates the role of students of the Virginia Military Institute in the Civil War and contains artifacts of Stonewall Jackson's life.

99. The Civil War at Endview
362 Yorktown Road
Newport News, Virginia 23603
(757) 887-1862
www.endview.org

Restored plantation house and grounds with exhibits on the Peninsular Campaign and the impact of the Civil War on American culture and society.

100. Lee-Hall Mansion
163 Yorktown Road
Newport News, VA 23603
(757) 888-3371
www.leehall.org

Antebellum mansion with exhibits that interpret the history of the Peninsular Campaign.

101. Blandford Church and Reception Center (The Petersburg Museums)
321 S. Crater Road
Petersburg, VA 23803
(804) 733–2400
www.petersburg-va.org

Commemorative exhibit of Confederate soldiers who fought in the Petersburg Campaign with a cemetery containing the graves of 30,000 Confederate soldiers.

102. Pamplin Historical Park and the National Museum of the Civil War Soldier
6125 Boydton Road
Petersburg, VA 23803
(804) 861–2408
www.pamplinpark.org

The site of the Union breakthrough during the siege of Petersburg commemorates the life of the average soldier during the Petersburg campaign.

103. Petersburg National Battlefield
1539 Hickory Hill Road
Petersburg, VA 23803
(804) 732-3531
www.nps.gov/pe_info.htm

A military museum is located on the site of the Petersburg battlefield, and activities include a 26-mile driving tour around the battle sites of General Grant's siege

104. Siege Museum (The Petersburg Museums)
15 W. Bank Street
Petersburg, VA 23803
(804) 733–2404
www.petersburg-va.com

Museum of the Civil War in Petersburg and on African-American history.

105. The Museum of the Confederacy
1201 E. Clay Street
Richmond, VA 23219
(804) 649–1861
www.moc.org

The museum features a collection of artifacts and documents pertaining to the Confederate States of America, including library and research facilities.

106. Richmond National Battlefield Park
3215 E. Broad Street
Richmond, VA 23223
(804) 226-1981
www.nps.gov/rich

Sites include the Chimborazo Medical Museum, the Civil War museum at the Tredgar Iron Works, and 11 battlefield sites from the Army of the Potomac's three attempts to capture Richmond, including Cold Harbor, Fort Harrison, Gaines' Mill, and Malvern Hill.

107. Harper's Ferry National Historical Park
Fillmore Street
Harper's Ferry, WV 25425
(304) 535–6224
www.nps.gov/hafe

The site of John Brown's 1859 raid on the federal arsenal, as well as the Potomac River crossing for the Confederate invasion of the North, the park includes the John Brown Museum, the Black Voices Museum, the Civil War museum, and exhibitions relating to the social and economic history of the Harper's Ferry community.

108. West Virginia Independence Hall
1528 Market Street
Wheeling, WVA 26003
(304) 238-1300

Museum depicting West Virginia history and statehood movement during the Civil War.

INDEX